Of a Comb, a Prayer Book, Sugar Cubes, & Lice:

Survivor of Six Concentration Camps
Elizabeth Blum Goldstein

Shana Fogarty

Edited by Maryann McLoughlin O'Donnell, Ph.D
A project of the Holocaust Resource Center
The Richard Stockton College of New Jersey
Cover Design by Ryan Schocklin

ComteQ
P U B L I
MARGATE, New Jersey

D0813832

Published by:
    ComteQ Publishing
    A division of ComteQ Communications, LLC
    P.O. Box 3046
    Margate, New Jersey 08402
    609-487-9000 • Fax 609-822-4098
    Email: publisher@ComteQcom.com
    Website: www.ComteQpublishing.com

ISBN 0-9766889-4-8
ISBN13 978-0-9766889-4-5
Library of Congress Control Number: 2005936381

Book design by Rob Huberman

Printed in the United States of America
10 9 8 7 6 5 4 3 2 1

This book is dedicated

To my grandmother,
Elizabeth Blum Goldstein.

To the memory of her family
and friends who perished.

To the six million Jews who were
murdered in the Holocaust.

To those who make an effort
to learn about what happened.

Anyone who closes his mind to the past is blind to the present...whoever refuses to remember the inhumanity is prone to new risks of infection.

—Richard von Weizsacker,
Former President of West Germany, 1985

Acknowledgements

I owe a special thank you to the many people in my life that helped me complete this project. Most importantly, I want to thank my grandmother, who not only endured the horrors of the Holocaust, but also relived those experiences as she struggled to share her personal and painful memories with me.

I also owe a huge thank you to Distinguished Professor of Holocaust Studies, Dr. Carol Rittner, R.S.M., who agreed to work with me to complete this project. I cannot convey how greatly appreciative I am of all the time and assistance she has given me.

My gratitude to the staff of the Holocaust Resource Center at The Richard Stockton College of New Jersey—to Gail Rosenthal, the Director, for her help in completing this project and to Maryann McLoughlin, my editor, for her comments and assistance in the many stages of publication. I also want to thank Dr. McLoughlin for introducing me to Professor Pam Hendricks who plans to write a drama based on my grandmother's story. I thank Pam Cross, Director of the Writing Center, who edited an early version of the manuscript. I am indebted to the Graphics Department at Stockton College—to Julie Bowen for her suggestions about the cover and especially to Ryan Schocklin for the author photograph as well as the cover design and title page. Thank you too to Maureen Sullivan who took photographs of the comb and prayer book for the cover page.

And to my family and friends, I must express my gratitude. They have provided me with the unconditional support, encouragement, and love needed to complete this project. My mother and father, Susan and Joseph Fogarty, have raised me to become the person that I am today. I owe my success to them. My brother and sister, Adam and Bryana Fogarty, continue to impact my life positively everyday. To my best friend, Jamie Riess, who has always been there for me, through thick and thin. I appreciate the friendship that we have more than I can put into words.

I also would like to thank everyone who expresses an interest in reading this book, in learning about the Holocaust, and in taking action against genocide.

Preface

Every student of the *Shoah* knows the critical importance of survivors' testimonies in reconstructing the crimes of the Nazis. They bring us as close as we are ever likely to get to the multifaceted essence of that terrible experience. That is why it is so important for us to encourage survivors to speak and write, to go back and re-member, to reconstruct for us and for future generations "the ruins" of their agonizing memories, memories they probably would rather "forget," if they could, but can't. The book you hold in your hand was written not by a survivor of the *Shoah* — the Holocaust — but by the granddaughter of a survivor.

Shana Fogarty is an exceptional young woman, sensitive and determined, committed to studying and remembering the *Shoah*, determined to carry the burden of being, like Elie Wiesel, a "messenger to humanity." Like Elie Wiesel, who, unknowingly, inspired and prodded Shana to encourage her Hungarian Jewish grandmother, Elizabeth Blum Goldstein, to speak and share her complex and painful memories with her granddaughter in a series of interviews, Shana Fogarty's message is a plea for peace in our world and understanding for survivors of the Holocaust. Shana wants people to learn about the Holocaust, to remember that horrific event in such a way that their remembering becomes, in Wiesel's words, "a shield" against such things happening again. She also wants the reader to recognize the quiet heroism and triumph of her grandmother's life, a life lived generously for family, friends, and community for these sixty plus years since the liberation of the last Nazi concentration camp in Europe. While Hitler and the Nazis destroyed so much that was precious to Elizabeth Blum Goldstein — family, friends, and community — they could not destroy her Jewish spirit, her Jewish heart, which she has passed on to her family, and most especially to her granddaughter Shana Fogarty.

Everyone who studies the *Shoah* is conscious that survivors often forget unpleasant facts and memories, repress or modify memories — it's a very human thing to do, particularly if one has been impacted by new information many years after a historical event. Shana lovingly encouraged her grandmother, Elizabeth Blum Goldstein to remember and to speak the "truth" about her experiences during the Holocaust, as clearly as her "Grandma" humanly could do. That is why *Of a Comb, a Prayer Book, Sugar Cubes, and Lice: Survivor of Six Concentration Camps—Elizabeth Blum Goldstein* makes interesting reading and will be part of the legacy of survival — during and after the *Shoah* — survivors leave to their families, and to us all.

Dr. Carol Rittner, RSM
Distinguished Professor, Holocaust & Genocide Studies
The Richard Stockton College of New Jersey

Table of Contents

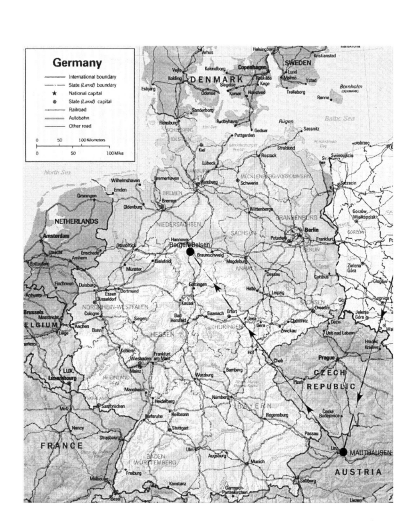

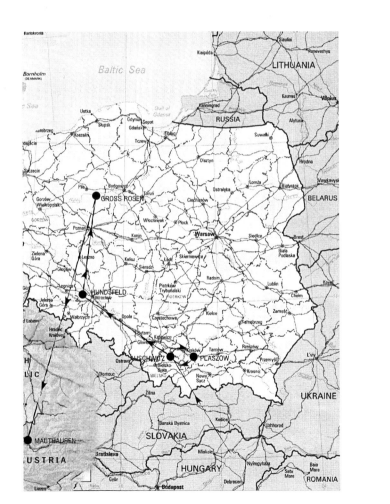

Introduction

Once there they put me in bed and then two nurses put me into a tub filled with hot water. I couldn't hear then and I couldn't speak either. Whatever they did to me they did. But I remember sitting in this tub and one nurse was holding both of my hands. The other one was using a big scrubbing floor brush, as if she had a very soiled floor and she needed to scrub it. And while I was sitting in this water she was pulling off all of the scabs, all those wounds that I had, and was cleaning them out with that brush. She had to because . . . there were lice living in them. I was screaming; I remember I was crying.

The above happened not during the Holocaust and was not done by the Nazis. It happened *after* my grandmother was liberated by the British army in April of 1945. This was a horror she had to endure as a result of the Holocaust.

The Holocaust

The Holocaust (1933-1945) literally changed the course of human history in that it wiped out Jewish communities all over Nazi-occupied Europe, destroying European Jewish culture and decimating the lives of millions of Jews, like my grandmother, who were guilty of nothing more that having been born Jewish in a world hostile to Jews and Judaism. Despite the fact that since 1945 thousands of books have been written in many languages about the Holocaust, that millions of extant Nazi documents have been preserved and cataloged in archives and research institutes, that thousands of Jews and non-Jews have freely spoken about what they witnessed and what they endured during the Holocaust, that Allied military personnel who entered the Nazi concentration and death camps and freed prisoners have testified to what they witnessed, some people deny that the Holocaust ever happened.

While I may not be able to change the minds of people who want to deny that the Holocaust happened, I can do something about contributing to the historical record by adding new evidence, based on the experiences of my 79-year-old grandmother, Elizabeth Blum Goldstein, who lived through the terrible Nazi years. I hope my work will help people of good will to remember the Holocaust and what happened to the Jews during that time.

Holocaust History

In studying the Holocaust, I have learned to keep a few important facts in mind. Specific dates and events are important for reasons of documentation and research. However, the values, concepts, and ideas that allowed the Holocaust to take place also need to be studied if we are to learn from the past for the sake of the future. We also need to be clear about what we mean when we speak of the *Holocaust*. As Susan Bachrach, author of *Tell Them We Remember*, writes:

> The Holocaust was the state-sponsored, systematic persecution and annihilation of European Jewry by Nazi Germany and its collaborators between 1933 and 1945. Jews were the primary victims—six million were murdered; Roma (Gypsies), the handicapped, and Poles were also targeted for destruction or decimation for racial, ethnic, or national reasons. Millions more, including homosexuals, Jehovah's Witnesses, Soviet prisoners of war, and political dissidents, also suffered grievous oppression and death under Nazi tyranny.

Hungary and the Holocaust

Every European country was affected by Nazi Germany and the Holocaust. Hungary was one of the hardest hit countries along with neighboring countries including Romania, Czechoslovakia, Yugoslavia, and Austria. In 1939, there were 403,000 to 445, 000 Jews in Hungary out of a population of 9.1 million. However, after acquiring former Czech and Romanian lands, the Jewish population jumped to about 700,000. The total Hungarian population rose to 15 million ("Hungary: General Survey"). The Jewish people who lived in Hungary were scattered throughout the country. My grandmother, Elizabeth Blum Goldstein, a Hungarian Holocaust survivor reflects, "We were all Hungarians, we just had different customs."

On January 30, 1933, Adolf Hitler, head of the Nazi Party in Germany, became Chancellor of Germany, the most powerful position in the German government. Hungary, located to the southeast of Germany, eventually developed an alliance with Nazi Germany. According to the *Encyclopedia of the Holocaust,*

> The Hungarians thought an alliance with Germany would be good for them because the two governments had similar authoritarian ideologies. They also knew the Germans could help them regain the land they had lost in World War I. Over the next five years Hungary moved ever closer to Germany. The Munich Conference of September 1938 allowed Germany to hand some of the land formerly lost to Czechoslovakia back into Hungarian hands. ("Hungary: General Survey")

In October 1940, Hungary joined the Axis alliance, allying itself with Nazi Germany, Fascist Italy, and Imperial Japan. Within a short time, Hungary adopted the anti-Jewish ideology of the Nazis, and soon the Hungarians put in place legal action against Jews in Hungary.

The country passed a law that cut Jewish participation in the economy and the professions by 80 percent. In May 1939 the Hungarian government limited the Jews even further in the economy and distinguished the Jews as a "racial" rather than religious group. In 1939 Hungary also created a new type of labor service draft which Jewish men of military age were forced to join. In 1941 the Hungarian government passed a racial law, similar to the Nuremberg laws, which officially defined who was to be considered Jewish. ("Hungary: Jews during the Holocaust")

During this time, Admiral Miklós Horthy was president and thus head of the Hungarian government. The Horthy regime, while antisemitic, did not want to deport or murder Jews.

In June 1941 Hungary decided to join Germany in its war against the Soviet Union. By December of that year, Hungary joined the Axis in declaring war against the United States. But after Germany's defeat at Stalingrad and other battles in which Hungary lost tens of thousands of its soldiers, Horthy began trying to back out of the alliance with Germany. ("Hungary: General Survey")

Hitler was well aware of Horthy's attempt to back out of Hungary's alliance with the Third Reich. On March 19, 1944, German troops invaded Hungary to keep the country loyal by force. Hitler immediately set up a new government that he thought would be faithful, with Dome Sztojay, Hungary's former ambassador to Germany, as prime minister. On October 15, Horthy announced publicly that he was finished with Hungary's alliance with Germany and was going to make peace with the Allies. The Germans blocked this move and then toppled Horthy's government, giving power to Ferenc Szalasi and his Fascist, violently antisemitic Arrow Cross Party. The Arrow Cross Party was similar to the SS and was made up of Hungarian Nazis who played a major role in the destruction of Hungarian Jews. According to *The Macmillan Encyclopedia of the Holocaust*, "Terror was rampant, with armed Arrow Cross gangs roaming the streets, robbing and killing Jews" ("Hungary").

Under the control of the Germans, the "Final Solution of the Jewish Question" was quickly implemented by Adolf Eichmann, a German Nazi officer charged with carrying out this project in

Hungary. The rights of all Hungarian Jews were immediately taken away. They could no longer own radios and telephones, which kept them from learning what was happening in the world beyond Hungary. Worse for them, as *The Encyclopedia of the Holocaust* states,

> Jewish property and businesses were seized, and the Jews of Hungary were forced into ghettos. After two to six weeks the Jews of each ghetto were put on trains and deported. Between May 15 and July 9, [1944] about 430,000 Hungarian Jews were deported, mainly to Auschwitz, where half were gassed on arrival. ("Hungary").

Despite the fear and destruction, groups of people made an effort to try to help the Jews of Hungary. Various Zionist Youth members and anti-Nazi parties saved many Jews by hiding them, giving them false documents, and providing them with food and shelter. Raoul Wallenberg, a Swedish diplomat, saved thousands of Jews in Budapest, Hungary. In "Swedish Portraits," Bulow explains:

> Wallenberg was born in 1912 to a prominent Swedish family. He studied in the United States at the University of Michigan for three and a half years and worked as a foreign representative for a central European trading company. In 1944, at the request of President Roosevelt and The United States' War Refugees Board, he was sent by the Swedish Foreign Minister to Budapest in an attempt to save the Jewish community of Budapest—the last left in Europe.
>
> Armed only with courage, determination, and imagination, Raoul Wallenberg saved approximately 100,000 Jews from slaughter. He was able to issue thousands of protective passes, purchase and maintain "safe houses" and soup kitchens, and secure food, medicine and clothing for the new "Swedish citizens" and the many children orphaned by the Nazi violence. A master of diplomacy, organization, threats, bribery and charm, he brought people back from death trains and death marches.

Although the efforts of these individuals and groups saved the lives of some Hungarian Jews, the *Encyclopedia of the Holocaust* notes that as many as "564,500 Hungarian Jews perished during the Holocaust" ("Hungary").

My grandmother's story

My grandmother, Elizabeth Blum Goldstein, a Hungarian Jew, did not perish. I believe it is important to tell the story of the Holocaust from the perspective of people like my grandmother. Of course, it is important to learn about World War II and the Holocaust from well-written and accurate books and by studying texts and other documents from that period. But when survivors share their stories, listeners cannot help but be deeply touched by the reality of what happened more than sixty years ago as a result of the actions of ordinary people like you and me. Oral histories are an essential record of events, made all the more urgent in the case of the Holocaust as time passes and survivors die and no longer bear witness.

The story of Hungarian Jewry during the Holocaust is filled with sadness. Hundreds of thousands of innocent people were murdered by the Germans and their collaborators in the concentration camps of Auschwitz and Birkenau, and few Hungarian Jews survived. Everyone who survived the Holocaust had a unique experience and each story is important for us to know and remember.

The story that follows is my grandmother's oral history. She was an ordinary Jewish woman from Hungary. She went through the Holocaust as a teenager, a very young woman. In my eyes, she is one of the strongest women alive today. She has shown more determination, perseverance, and drive than anyone else I have ever met.

She refused to die, and if she hadn't been so stubborn, I would not be here today to tell her story.

From my youngest years and my earliest memories of my

grandmother, I can say that she has been warm and friendly to everyone in her life. My grandma treats everybody equally. She cares about family, friends, and the good of all people. But behind her smile there is a sadness that has haunted her for six decades. She has memories that are so unbearable that she becomes physically ill when she recalls what happened to her. Very few people have been able to tap into the events that happened to her during the Holocaust, nor have they known just how these memories devastated her once happy life, but I have been privileged to hear her secrets.

My grandmother has allowed me to ask her questions about her life in Hungary before the war and during the Holocaust. I have seen her tears and experienced what she goes through when she talks about her past. Sometimes I felt horrible causing her to relive these long-ago experiences. Sometimes I just wanted to hold her hand, hug her, and tell her everything is okay. However, everything isn't okay, and nothing can be done to change that, but I can let her know that I love her, that I want to learn from her, and that I want to share her story with others, so that more people will learn what *genocide* means. Then perhaps more people will stand up and say, "We must stop genocide!"

Interview Process

To complete this project of interviewing my grandmother, we met and tape-recorded our conversations. I did have a notebook but I took very few notes. When I was writing up the interview, I played the tape recorder, stopping and starting it as I typed. We met on four different occasions in my grandmother's home, and each interview lasted for about an hour. It was just too difficult to talk about her painful memories for much longer than that. Here, then, is my grandmother, Elizabeth Blum Goldstein's story. She shared it with me, and now I share it with you so that together we can learn from the past for the sake of the future.

Statement of Purpose

Elizabeth Blum Goldstein stated her purpose in agreeing to the interview as follows:

I wanted to put my story into words. It was very difficult for me to recall this horrible part of my life, but I felt I needed to tell my children and grandchildren what happened.

Interview #1

Sunday June 20, 2004

When and where were you born?

I was born Elizabeth Blum in Hungary on March 19, 1926. The name of the town was Kisar, 40 kilometers (about twenty miles) from Mátészalka, the nearest city (see map page 62). I was born and I grew up there until we were ordered out. I had a very normal family life; we were a big family. We were eight children. I had an older brother, and I was the second child, the oldest girl. So there were a lot of things that I had to do that were pretty grown up. I almost could say that I was never a child because my mom depended on me very much to help out. I helped raise the children and prepare meals for the family. We didn't have ready-made things like here, where you go to the supermarket and buy a box of pasta. We had to make the pasta first and that took hours. After we made the pasta, which I can still do today, we had to roll it out and then let it dry and cut it to the width we wanted it to be. So it was a project, even breakfast: we didn't have instant coffee; we had no coffee makers; we had to grind the coffee first and then cook it. We had our own way of making the food. And then came dinnertime and yet another project.

I had little sisters and brothers and my mother was usually busy. My father was always busy with our store, so they depended on me so much that I really couldn't participate in things that my friends were doing like riding their bicycles or going to the library to borrow books. I never had time for that. Sometimes I was a bit resentful but I never showed it; I did everything cheerfully. Sometimes I just thought it wasn't really fair. But then I explained to myself that it's because we were a very large family; we were the largest of all the families that we were friendly with. I had the most siblings, you know sisters and brothers; I had five brothers and two sisters.

Do you remember their names?

Sure I remember their names. My oldest brother was Sándor; he was two years older than me. I was just about eighteen years old when the Germans invaded Hungary and our lives changed forever. And then I had a younger brother who was 16. His name was Miklos. That's the brother that lives in Israel. After Miklos was my sister Ibolya. She was about twelve or thirteen years old at the time. After Ibolya was my brother David and then Miriam. Actually Miriam's Hungarian name was Magda. And then I had two brothers that were very close in age. My brother Zoltan was about six years old and my little brother Samuel was four years old. You know I have to think about it all. When I was in Sweden after everything happened, I started realizing that I must remember my past; I wrote some things down in a book.

Do you still have it?

I have the book; actually it's a prayer book we were given after the war.   I have everybody's name and birthday recorded and I was grateful for that because I wanted to make so sure that I remembered it all. (see page 68)

So we have Sándor, you, Miklos, Ibolya, David, Magda, Zoltan, and Samuel?

Yes.

What was your town like?

Kisar was a small town in Hungary. My father was born there and we owned a business.

What kind of business?

It was like a general store. We also had orchards of fruit trees and wheat that we grew. People were working for my father; you know, my father was a wonderful man. And that's how we made a living. But the atmosphere was always very serious as long as I can remember. I kind of knew that the grown-ups were troubled, and I was always listening in on their conversations. I remember knowing that times were very difficult. I also went to school.

How long did you go to school?

Actually, I was not allowed to go to a *gymnasium* (a high school)—by this time no Jews could attend public schools. I would have gone to a *gymnasium* in another city, but wasn't allowed. However, because I was smart, my parents hired a tutor and I attended private school with a few other Jewish children. I did go to the big city school to graduate. However, I don't remember getting a diploma at all; we knew already that we probably were not even on the list. But we went through the whole thing anyway.

After this, I just stayed home and helped my family. I helped my mom, and I really did everything, everything you can think of that a grown person would have to do while owning a house and having a family. I cooked, I baked, I cleaned the house, and sometimes I really didn't like that. But I did it and I would do it again. That was natural I guess. There was no diaper service; we had to wash the diapers and use them again. We had to boil them so they were sanitized and this was a lot of work. I don't even remember a baby carriage in the house; I used to carry my little sister and brother on my hip. It was really something else, but those are my memories and I can't paint them better.

My mom was very excitable; she was always busy. I remember her saying, "When I finish breakfast, I have to start lunch!" And this was very true. All in all I had a lovely family, a loving family. My parents were very good to each other; there were no fights. The kids had fights amongst themselves but we just tried to live as normally as possible. And it wasn't easy.

What were your parents' names?

My mother's name was Hannah; her maiden name was Braun. And my father's name was Martin Blum.

So when they got married she became Hannah Blum?

Yes. Your mom was named after my mother, whose Hebrew name was Hannah. Your mother's Hebrew name is Hannah.

Does she know that?

Yes. And my son's name is Marta, that's after my father. And you're named after Elona's mother (Elona is my grandmother's first cousin).

That's her name too, Shana?

Shandel. Her name was Charlotta, Charlotte.

Interesting. So were you pretty close to your family?

Yes, we were very close.

Did you have to work in the store?

Oh yes, whenever there were customers I worked in the store. The only thing I never did was work in the field; we had workers for that. We had a lot of land and orchards where we had fruit, walnuts, vegetables, and all sorts of things growing. And other people cultivated that. I remember I used to get on my bicycle, and sometimes I had to try to find my father to bring him lunch.

So those were the things I did. There was no social life; it was just the everyday needs. We tended to them, but I used to think that we didn't really know any better. I was always listening, and I was always wondering why we settled in such a small town. Maybe if we lived in a big town it would have been more interesting. But that's what it was.

Did you have lots of friends at school?

Some, yes, some. We walked to the public school.

And did you have regular classes?

Yes, sure, very limited, you know. It's amazing that I did as well as I did because we didn't have really good teachers; it was almost like a two-room school. The same teacher taught different classes for the younger people and for the older people. It was primitive, very primitive. I always liked to learn, and I didn't think some things that were done were really right. Sometimes in the higher grade the boys had to go look for the teacher. He would go into a bar and have a couple drinks about midday. We were left alone.

The teacher would drink?

Yes, it was not well disciplined. But that's what it was.

While you were in school you noticed things changing? Was it before the Nazis invaded Hungary?

Yes, around the time of the things I was talking about before. I was very young and I remember helping my mother bake bread, I must have been ten or twelve years old. These are the memories I have from that time, but mine wasn't a happy carefree childhood. We didn't go anywhere, and I knew that there were problems, the grown-ups knew. People had radios, nobody had television, but people had radios and heard the news. And there was the newspaper, I remember my father read the paper and was discussing it with my mother, and I was listening; I always listened. We heard the rumors.

Hitler invaded Hungary; actually he was invited by the Hungarian government in 1944 to occupy the country. But these bad things had actually already started in 1938. I was only twelve years old, and I knew the grownups heard rumors about what was happening in other countries like Poland and elsewhere. And in order to cope most people just said, "This can't be; it's probably people making things up; it just can't be." That's the way people survived. And then there were more and more rumors, and as I said before, I was aware.

I was very concerned, and I remember feeling almost a depression, knowing what was happening, and always worrying, what if it's really true? What if this is all true, what's going to become of us? So I used to talk to my father all the time. He was a very calm man. He was also a very tall man and my mother was a short girl, but they were wonderfully matched. I would come to my father and say, "I know what you were talking about, and I want to know what's going to become of us. What do we do?" And he would put his hand on my head and say, "Don't worry about anything, nothing is going to happen to us; we are good citizens, we have done nothing wrong. Don't worry about it." And that would always make me feel good until I heard these things again; it never took long. I would ask him over and over again, and he would always reassure me that nothing would go wrong because we didn't deserve anything bad. He'd say not to worry about it, but I did; I knew.

And then one day we were preparing for Passover at someone's house. We baked our own matzo, so we were working on that when somebody came to the door. I'll never forget this. It was March 1944, and by then the Jewish people did not own radios. They gave them up because people accused them of listening to Russian stations and Communists. Then they'd take away the family, and you would never see them again. Or they just took away the head of the family and that was the end of them. So nobody owned radios, so they couldn't accuse us of listening to them. It was word of mouth from one town to another. People got to others by bicycle; nobody owned cars. But somebody came and told us, I remember, as we were preparing the matzos, somebody came and said that Hitler just came into Hungary. I remember us like dropping dead. It was as if the strength went out of everybody, and I remember watching the faces and I knew that something was really, really bad. And it really was.

They made us wear yellow stars so we would stand out in the crowd. We had to wear it on the outer garment. They didn't give it to us; we had to make it. I remember I cut out cardboard and covered it with yellow cloth. And we just knew that things were not good. This went on for a couple of weeks and we tried to survive, but there were a lot of restrictions. Even in our store, they forced us to be open on the holiday (the *Sabbath*, the Jewish day of worship and rest, from sundown Friday to sundown Saturday); they did this on purpose. So the store was open, but some of the neighbors knew that we were traditional Jews and they didn't come in because of the *Sabbath*. And some people didn't know, they thought they could buy things, and we told them the store was open but we weren't selling anything. We took chances; if we were reported we certainly would pay for this bitterly.

These memories stand out in my mind; I was a youngster at

that time. I can tell you about my family, my town, where we came from. And then not long after that, maybe two or three weeks later, Nazis were gathering all the people from Hungary. I remember I used to ask my father, "Could you talk to your friends, the ones you went to school with, and the mayor, or anyone else who has a position?" And he said they didn't want to talk to him. They probably were afraid, mostly afraid that they were going to get into trouble. They were afraid to mingle with Jewish people because then they would not be doing what was expected of them.

And so there was no one to turn to, Shana. There was no government to turn to. No single person to turn to. I remember my father was drafted; I was very young, maybe nine or ten years old. He was drafted into the army, but they didn't give him a uniform. He had to wear his own clothes and he was taken into a labor-like camp instead of the army. He was supposed to be like a soldier. And this appointed Hungarian officer who was their commander in chief was telling people that the Hungarian government was doing a terrible thing to the Jewish people. And he wasn't Jewish. But he said, "They are putting sand in your eyes so you don't see the real truth now that Hitler is in Hungary." I don't know what happened to him, but, you see, sometimes there were some people that spoke up.

I remember when we were ordered out of our home. There were Hungarian policemen that were appointed to remove us. They came to the house and told us to pack everything up. Well, not to pack everything, but take something with us, what we could carry. And I remember I went in and took several of my blouses out from the closet and put them all on me because that was easier to do. They put us on this horse and buggy to take us to a ghetto, another city, Mátészalka, pretty far away (see map page 62). And one of our neighbors, I'll never forget this; she lived next door with family a couple of houses away from us. She came out with a couple of freshly baked breads and put them next to us. That was very sweet. But not everybody was like that; I remember somebody was yelling, "Make sardines out of them." So these things stand out in my mind. We were taken on the wagon for hours and were brought into a big city in Hungary. That's where they brought all the families from my district.

What was the name of the city where you were taken?

Mátészalka.   I knew we were in trouble, and again I questioned my father, and he said, "We'll be okay, they'll send us home in no time. You know they're probably going to question you a little bit and then we'll go home." And I believed it; you know, I wanted to believe it.

How long did the trip take on horse and buggy?

Several hours, maybe five or six hours. And I remember we had a little dog, and the dog was running after us as we pulled away from our house because he was a part of our family. He was running, running, and then one of those officers shot him. And I remember the only thing I had; you know we had no toys and games, so we had to make our own—we drew boxes in the street and jumped in them (hop scotch). The same with crayons and all that, nobody had "bought" games. I had one rag doll that I shared with my sister. But I had a bicycle and that was a real prestigious thing to have. And I had to leave it, they didn't let me take it, and I remember I said to myself, "No bicycle." That was my only treasure, if I had time, to ride the bicycle.

They took us to this place that was part of the city, but it was barricaded. People arrived from all directions and we had to make a home there. We had a room in an attic with four other families. There was no privacy. I don't even know how we survived it but we did. And I think they had a soup kitchen every once in a while. I don't remember much about that. I tried to play with the kids to keep them quiet; after all I had little sisters and brothers and we tried to be as normal as possible. We were thinking that this is just temporary and then we are going to go back and pick up our lives again, which never happened.

Interview #2

Saturday, June 26, 2004

Do you remember anything about your grandparents?

I remember especially my paternal grandfather because he lived with us. He had his own room, and I used to go in and talk to him or just look in on him. He died in 1937; I was very young, maybe about eleven. But still I remember him. He was an elderly man already. Maybe he was about 82 when he died, and that was really old in those days. I only heard about my grandmother. I think I was just two years old when she died. I don't remember anything about her.

I remember somewhat my mother's mother because I used to visit my mother's hometown, Csenger, sometimes in the summertime. My mother and father would send me there. I always got a ride from somebody, and I would spend a few weeks in the summertime at my uncle's with my cousins. That was a big deal for me because it was unusual. So I remember my grandmother.

I also remember that same grandmother came to live with us at one time temporarily because my mother was very ill. And I remember there were five of us. And she cooked for us, but she wasn't very happy because she didn't know how to handle a whole family. So that wasn't very pleasant. I remember my brother used to get very angry with her. It was a strange thing that she cooked and then she said she didn't want to give it to us because she said she then has to cook again. And I think my brother who now lives in Israel, he was a little boy, he probably wouldn't even remember this. He picked up a stick or something and told her, "If you don't give it to me, I'm going to hit you."

Oh my goodness!

He was very hungry and grandma wasn't very reasonable. But I remember these things, I wasn't part of it. I was never much for food. I was very, very skinny but whatever there was was fine with me. But now that you are asking, it comes into my mind. And so we didn't have much to do. In other words, these were the very early years, and in the later years they were gone. But I had uncles and I had cousins in my mother's hometown, Csenger.

Csenger? Is that the town where they were from?

Yes, that's the name of the town—in Hungary.

Did you get to see your cousins and uncles a lot?

Once in a while in the summertime I'd see them for a little while. They never came to us. I was just sent, I think my mother felt I should get away for a little bit, so I would go and just hang out. I didn't really do anything. I feel very bad that I can't show you a picture of your great grandparents.

You don't have to feel bad, just hearing about them is important. Let's talk about when you were in Hungary. You mentioned a little bit about the government and how something wasn't right with it. What do you remember about the government and what was it like when you lived in Hungary?

Well, I was very alert and was always listening to the grown ups when they exchanged news. Hitler was ruling since around 1933, I believe. Hungary was starting to go along with the same kind of rules toward the Jewish people as the Germans. The Hungarians made laws. They brought in laws so the Jewish people would get choked out of society. For example, we had to write down our ethnicity when we applied for a license, no matter what type of license. Whether opening a store or for any kind of business, we needed a license. If you were Jewish, however, you couldn't get one. As soon as your ethnicity was registered as Jewish, that was it. Most Jewish people eat kosher meat, especially in Europe, but the Hungarians passed a law that people couldn't do kosher slaughtering, which meant that the Jewish people couldn't eat meat.

Later on, we couldn't go to school. Or, we could go, but we couldn't graduate. My parents had a private teacher for me at home. And when I went to graduation in the city, I found out I wasn't graduating. I just was there. And we couldn't complain to anybody because this was the government. So we turned to our best friends and our neighbors. We knew just about everybody because my father had been born in that town and went to school with people who had positions in the town. They just shrugged their shoulders and said they couldn't do anything, and they wouldn't do anything. They were afraid to be in touch, so to speak, or to show friendship because Hitler was so very cruel. They also taxed us for a lot of things; they found ways of antagonizing and taking things such as our rights away from us. We had our store, and they would come in and find fault with it. Or, they made us stay open on the Sabbath, on Saturday, when we would never have been open.

There were all sorts of signs and I remember, although I was young, maybe about ten or eleven years old, I saw that my parents were scared and frightened. I was just as frightened, and I remember the feeling of wondering how we would eat. How would we go on? There were eight children, ten people in the family, and it was a very serious situation. Unfortunately, I was very much aware of everything and I suffered because of that.

The first place that you were taken when you were taken from your home was Mátészalka. Tell me a little more about that.

Yes. That was a city where part of it was blocked off, and they brought the Jewish families from all around the area and from other counties. The accommodations were horrible. We brought some food with us, some. I remember we had a lot of sugar cubes and some bread. But we were gathered there, in such terrible accommodations, just horrible. There were several families in an attic or in a room; there was no privacy, nothing. And nobody knew what was going on. We were not allowed to go out and nobody was allowed to come in. Nobody spoke to us to tell us anything, to explain or give hope, or to help understand actually what was going on.

Again I was always watching my parents and the grown-ups, and I knew that we were in trouble, but nobody talked about it because we had to hope that this was temporary. People tried to believe that because otherwise they just couldn't function at all. We stayed in this place about four to six weeks, something like that. We stayed without knowing what our future was, why we were there, if we were going to go home, or when.

Where was this place in Hungary?
Mátészalka was about 50-70 miles from my house.

So you just lived there with other families, not really doing anything?
Yes, just nothing, nothing, there was nothing to do. We were frightened and were hoping every day that something would happen, and we'd come to some sort of a decision.

So you didn't have to work or anything?
No, not as I remember. I don't know about the grown-ups; there must have been some sort of a kitchen somewhere. I don't really remember getting food there, but there must have been something that was given out once in a while. So we just stayed there and waited. And then one day after several weeks we were told that we were going to a different place. We had to take whatever we could with us because we were taken on foot. We weren't transported.

We arrived at a place that was like a train station. But it wasn't a train for people. They were wagons that were used to transport cows and horses. They had no windows; they had only a few little slits for air. You couldn't look out and you couldn't look in, but that's how the air would come in for the animals to breathe. Oh God, this is so hard for me to talk about.

Now there were German soldiers walking around with German shepherds. They were holding onto the German shepherds. And it took many hours when the soldiers ordered people onto these wagons. I saw they were bringing out people on stretchers, on folding chairs. Those were people, Jewish people, who had been pulled out of hospitals. They wanted everybody to be gotten rid of. These were dying people; it was horrible. And they ordered us on these trains. We got on the trains and then there was no room. We were like sardines standing up. There were no seats. We were all standing up. And there was no room. Then somebody yelled out, "There is no room in here!" And the German soldier let go of the German shepherd and ordered him to jump in and jump on us, and of course we all just backed off and got even tighter and he said, "You see you have room." And then they shoved in a couple of chairs with dying people on them.

They put a pail, an open pail in the corner and they said, "This is your toilet." That was for everybody. Just right in the corner. Then they locked the doors. And we were traveling about three days. Three days and nights. We never got off that train. The door was never opened.

There was no food or water at all?

No. I remember I had some sugar cubes in my pocket. No water, nothing. And it was very, very hot. People were screaming that they were dying, that they couldn't breathe. And I remember that I was trying to make room for those people so they could get closer to that opening where the slits were so they could catch some air. I felt strongly that I could do without that. But I remember the horrible sounds. I wasn't aware that the people were losing their minds. They were so upset. We were locked in—the doors were never opened—and we had no food, no water. And it was horrible.

When we first got on this train, I asked my father, "What's happening? What is going to become of us?" Before he had always said not to worry. He used to put his hand on my head and say, "We are good citizens, we didn't commit any crimes. This is just wartime and formalities. In no time we'll be home again and we'll be a family as we were."

And I remember when the door closed on us, and I snuggled up to my father and I asked him the question again. I said, "Daddy, what's happening, what's going to become of us?"

And I still see his face. He said to me, "I don't know anymore." And that's when I lost all my hopes, all my everything that kept me going. I no longer had anybody to turn to because my father said he no longer knew. And that stays with me.

We traveled. There was no food. I never remember eating anything. Three days and nights we went through tunnels, and this was a slow way of going. This was like a horse transport. And we arrived to a place where they . . . oh, Shana, it's so hard for me to tell you these things.

Do you want to stop? We can stop if you want.

No, I just want to tell you good things. And this is not good, not good at all.

We can stop.

No. We arrived and we didn't know where. We were just ordered off the wagon, and they said, "Just keep moving." We kept walking, and then I saw a wrought iron sign. I have seen it many times since on films and on television. *Arbeit Macht Frei*, "work makes free." Music was playing, I guess to cover up the sadness of what really was going on there. We came; we stayed together as a family, I remember very closely, as closely as we could.

As we were walking, we passed a woman lying on the ground. She was lying on the ground on her back, crying, screaming, and moaning. We looked at her and recognized her from the next town over from ours. We knew her family; she was the wife of our rabbi. She had four little children all around her crying. She was lying on the ground giving birth; she was begging for help, asking everybody. And we were ordered, "*Schnell. Schnell.*" "Quickly. Quickly." Nobody could help her. And then I heard a shot. Another prisoner confirmed that they had shot her. They let her give birth right on the street, and then they shot her.

Many years later when I was living in America, I met up with the rabbi I had known from Hungary. He asked if I knew if his wife had survived, or what happened to her. I told him I didn't know anything; I didn't have the heart to tell him what happened.

After we passed the rabbi's wife in Auschwitz, we walked for quite a while and then came up to these long tables where Germans were sitting. Here, they registered us. The Germans kept such an accurate record of what they were doing that later on this became handy to backtrack to find some of the things we needed to know. The Germans asked everyone's name, age, and other things as well.

Because of their age, the younger children usually held hands with a parent or an older sibling. I held hands with my younger sister who was thirteen years old. And after they registered us they made us go in different directions. I remember my mother; they ordered her to the right. She had four children with her. The younger children held onto her, and she was sent to the right. Later I learned that she was sent to the gas chamber with the younger children, right then and there. That was the end of them, but I didn't know it at the time. And my father, my older brother, and my younger brother were sent to walk straight. I remember that I took some sugar cubes out of my pocket and ran to my father and put them into his pocket. I remember that, and that was the last time I ever saw them. I was ordered to the left with my younger sister.

Your younger sister Ibolya?

Yes, Ibolya. She was thirteen years old at the time. We had to walk a little distance and as we came to the left; we came to a big warehouse. In that warehouse I remember being close to the door; we were shaved. Our heads were shaved and all body hairs were shaved. We were so humiliated. I remember my sister who was so young, she was so frightened. I assured her that we would be okay, not to be afraid. I think there was a shower outside that we had to go under. And then they handed us a dress, the same thing for everybody. They gave us a grey cotton dress and a pair of wooden shoes, clogs. We had to leave everything of our own in that warehouse. And we spent quite a bit of time there; we didn't know what was happening. Finally, they ordered us into these barracks, which were also not far from where we were. We had to walk everywhere.

Nobody spoke with us. I remember my sister was so frightened; I was too, but I couldn't show it to her. I tried to be strong. There too people were screaming, going crazy because we were locked in this big room. No food was given to us; I don't know how we managed, but we did. We had no food, no water. And we spent the night in this place sitting on a dirt floor. We were so scared; we had no one to talk to. Some rumors started that from here we would go to meet our parents. That was always a big lift, hoping that somebody knew something. We held onto that. But it didn't happen that way.

The next day they ordered us to go on some trains. Some sort of a train, packed very tightly with people. We were riding on the train, not knowing where we were going. We were taken to Plaszow, a town near Krakow, Poland, a bigger city that's better known (see map pages 5&6 and 62).[1] Sure enough we had arrived at a concentration camp. There were barbed wires all around. We were counted and were allowed to go into some barracks with bunk-like beds. There was no mattress, no blanket, no nothing; just layered wood for a bed. And I remember being so tired by then that I just felt I could no longer go or do anything. I just couldn't exist anymore.

So the first place you were taken to was Auschwitz, Poland, and then you were taken to Plaszow.

Yes.

How long did it take you to arrive in Plaszow from Auschwitz?

A couple of days.

Was that trip similar to the first trip?

Not quite, because we were taken on something like a train. It wasn't like a luxury train, but it had windows. I don't know how we went to the bathroom even; there was no bathroom. So we arrived to this horrible place. I was completely exhausted, but I was always looking after my sister.

The next day we had to get up very early. I think they gave us some black coffee in the morning and maybe a piece of bread. And we had to stand for hours to be counted in rows. And then they ordered us to work. In the camp where we were there was

the *Lager Kommandant*.   "*Lager*" means camp.   The camp
commander lived in a big white house. And we were ordered to
build him a swimming pool. We had to carry these huge rocks
and water and cement on our shoulders. And this was every day;
I was there for about five weeks. We did this work every day.
Rocks, cement, and water. And the *Lager Kommandant* would sit
on his porch-like patio with buckets of stones, and he'd aim them
at us as we walked by. We got hit lots of times. There was a
German soldier with a whip at the end of the road, and if we
didn't carry big enough rocks, then we got it from him. This work
was unbearable, it was so hot; the month was June. It was so hot,
we had no water. We would come back to our place at night, and
then we had to stand in line again to be counted.

One day they announced that if one person were missing,
every fifth person would be shot. And, of course, I was horrified
because I was afraid I would see my sister shot because someone
was missing; that was not in my control.   Those fears were
indescribable. I remember being so tired; a lot of people died
there.   I remember having the feeling sometimes that maybe
tomorrow I would be one of those people, and I wouldn't have to
do this anymore, you know, it would all end. But it didn't work
that way and I was there until the beginning of September 1944.

I also want to tell you that this man, this camp commandant
who was stoning us, I saw him many times from the barracks
beat up men, mostly men that were walking outside. This man
would come up, usually riding his white horse, and he would
get off the horse and kick the person until he died. Or, he just
kicked them from the horse. I saw him order some men to lie
down on their stomachs on the dirt floor and walk on their
elbows. They had to drag themselves along on their elbows. I
saw him beating, beating, punching, punching, punching until
the person just went limp. He was a cruel, cruel man. After
five miserable weeks, I recall something that somebody said
about some special people that were taken out of a place
nearby and had it much better than we did. That had to be
the people that made Schindler's list. The film that was made

shows that that's where the factory was, in Krakow. That's where Schindler got those men whom he protected in a way; it's what *Schindler's List* was based on. I was on the outside of Krakow in the concentration camp in Plaszow. For me, I just heard about something like that going on, but I wasn't a part of it.

I was getting thinner and thinner; I knew I didn't have much strength. But I played strong for my sister. I forever told her that we must stay alive; we must stay well because everybody would be home but us if we didn't hang on. Somehow I felt a certain stubbornness; I wouldn't let them destroy me. Then, in the beginning of September 1944, they made us get on these trains, again with miserable accommodations. And they took us back to Auschwitz.

Do you remember what month and what year you were taken from your home, and what month you were in the first place, Mátészalka?

We were taken from our home in April 1944. We were in the ghetto from April until June, about two months.

Okay, and how long were you in Auschwitz at first, just a day?

Just one day and then I came back in September.

So after you were in Auschwitz for a day you were taken to Plaszow?

Yes, I was taken to Plaszow near Krakow in the very beginning of June and stayed until the beginning of September 1944.

Okay. So then it was the beginning of September 1944 when you were taken from Plaszow.

Yes, we were taken back to Auschwitz.

And was that train ride similar to the second one?
Yes, similar.

Do you know about how long it took?
It took a couple of days. And then we were put into barracks there too.

Did you know when you got back there that you were back at the same place?

Yes.

You were put into barracks?

Yes. I must have been there for only a day or two when then they ordered us out of the barracks and tattooed our arms. We had to go to this place and again we stood in line. They tattooed a number on my arm that was B-737. And then when we got back in the barracks they ordered us back because they made a mistake. A half hour had gone by and they had to redo it. So we went back and on that painful area they crossed out the B. My arm was so swollen and painful. This tattoo is not like the kids get today cosmetically. This is down to the bone. I know this because I consulted a dermatologist a long time ago because I thought I wanted to remove it so nobody would remember and nobody would ask me questions. The doctor said it would really require surgery; I would have to go to the hospital and they would have to scoop out down to the bone and then pull it back together. I'd probably have a scar anyhow.

So when we went back they crossed out the B and they added A-20 to the 737. A-20737. It was a horrible experience but by then it was just another part of everything. I knew we were in trouble, and I remember feeling like a zombie. I actually couldn't really function anymore, from the hunger and the tiredness; I was not really functioning. Shana, I want to tell you that they gave us some sort of a fluid concoction called soup. And on the top of that little bowl of soup were worms swimming all over. It was supposed to be cabbage or something. But we were so hungry by that point that we just closed our eyes so we didn't see what we were eating. At least we were eating something. And they put some sort of drug in the liquid so none of the girls had periods.*

---

* In the concentration camps menstruation often stopped when the woman's body fat was low. After the Holocaust when they were eating a normal diet and enough calories, their body fat increased and then their periods resumed.

We had no underwear, none. We just had that one single dress. Every morning we had to stand in line to be counted, naked. They made us stand on the street with our dress and our shoes in our hand so we could be counted. It took hours. This was done every day by SS soldiers, German soldiers. Can I tell you how humiliating that was? They were looking for blemishes; they were looking for any kind of imperfection. Sometimes they selected people who had blemishes, and they pulled them out of the group and put them someplace else. And one day somehow my sister got separated from me, although we were always standing next to each other. She went to the right, and I saw that I had lost her. The soldiers were watching us with their guns drawn. She was just pushed to the side, and I got very, very upset and I ran after her with my dress in one hand and my shoes in the other. I knew I would never make it because I'd be shot but I didn't care. But somehow they didn't see it; there were a lot of people there. I took her back because I didn't know where they were planning on sending us. Somehow we came back, and I told her that from then on when they were counting us, she should not look up. I would shove her the way I wanted her to go. She'd be close to me, and I would maneuver so that she stayed with me. And that's how we'd stay together.

It was just so humiliating. I stayed in Auschwitz like a zombie, both of us, all of us, thinking of food all the time. Food and water were such a preoccupation that we just couldn't think about anything else, just food, something to eat. I was very hungry, very, very hungry all the time. They gave us some black coffee or this concoction of liquid and a piece of bread at the end of the day. But other than that we weren't doing anything, just walking around, lying around; nobody knew anything.

So you didn't have to do work or anything?

No, we just stood in line every day. We were on the street being counted, naked, it was horrible. I was there until about the middle of October, about a month or five weeks had gone by. One day, around the middle of October, after being counted again, they ordered us onto some transportation. It was some sort of a train that had no top, like you would take produce or something in it. Again we traveled for a few days and we wound up in Germany. Auschwitz was in Poland, remember, but this time we wound up in Germany in the town of Hundsfeld.[2] Here they put us into these buildings that had something like bunk beds. It was like heaven because we had a blanket, a thin blanket, but we felt that we were finally treated humanely. They assigned us to work in an ammunition factory to make ammunition for the Germans. I was ordered to make bullets in this factory. And unfortunately they separated us. My sister had to work the night shift, and I worked the day shift.

Was she making bullets too or did she do something else?

Maybe other people did other things but my group was working in this factory making ammunition for the Germans. And of course, again we were very exhausted. They woke us up very early in the morning. We had to stand in line to be counted again. After hours of standing in line we had to walk to work. As we walked, we saw some houses, people lived around there. I don't know how they didn't do anything about anything; people knew what was going on. I remember as we were taken we were just so hungry. I remember that we saw some Germans, and we were yelling to them that we were hungry. So they knew about us, but I don't know how much they knew or how much they wanted to know. We weren't hidden. We were very visible.

So people knew what was going on.

Absolutely. As I said we were working in a factory making ammunition. And I knew that the ammunition would be used against people whom I didn't want to hurt. So I sabotaged the work. I didn't make them the way I was supposed to. We were supposed to pick up a circular metal disk with a magnet and put it on top of the bullet before the machine closed it. If two or more were put on, it wouldn't work. So I put on two or more. Most of the time I got away with doing this, but I also got caught. They came; they knew we couldn't be trusted. So they came and pulled off rows of the bullets and there were lots of them that had more than one disk on them. I got so beat up that I lost my hearing for long time. I was beaten in the face by a female soldier, a German soldier.

There was another female soldier; I still remember her name was Helen. And she said to us that she was so sorry that she didn't really want to do what she was doing but she had to. She felt very sorry for us. And I remember thinking that when I got free and went back to Hungary, I would come back to Germany and I'd look up Helen. I would bring her to Hungary and I'd treat her so well and be so good to her because at least she said she was sorry. But the other woman, a short little soldier, hit me in the face so many times that I lost my hearing for the longest time. Her I would not bring to Hungary!

You lost your hearing totally?
Yes. My ear was clogged; I had no hearing.

For how long was it gone?
Oh, I don't know. I don't remember. I can't recall. It was a long time.

And then it just gradually came back?
Yes. It took a long time. Every day we went to work. We still felt that this was a better place to be than the places we had been to before. One day I found a metal comb on the street as we were walking to work. I picked it up and kept it with me. Everybody had been completely shaven, but by then, the girls' hair had started to grow back a little bit. It was only half an inch or an inch, but I started to style their hair with that one comb. The other girls wanted me to do something with their hair, and somehow I felt that I knew what to do. Of course I could only use spit for setting lotion. I remember that I was so popular because I could fix the girls' hair so they didn't look like nothing.

I spent quite a bit of time in Hundsfeld, from about the middle or end of October 1944 until the middle of January 1945. It was cold; it was snowing; it was windy; and we wore only that one cotton dress. One night I was "home," and my sister was in the factory. She worked at night, and we heard a tremendous noise outside. We didn't know what happened, and then we saw light, it was like daylight, but it was in the middle of the night. There were floaters in the air; they call them Russian candles I think. They lit up the whole place because we were being discovered by Americans—Russians, I don't know—maybe it was Belgian soldiers. They wanted to see what was going on, and they bombed the factory. They knew it was an ammunition factory. You can imagine how I felt, my sister was in the factory, and we heard the bombs falling all over; it was horrendous. But the people inside the factory were all taken down to a shelter with the Germans; they didn't leave the young people in the factory. She was saved. The next day we were told that we had to leave because we had been discovered.

We were told to stand in line because we would be leaving. This was in the middle of January 1945. We weren't allowed to take anything from the room, not even the blankets. We were ordered to line up, four in a row. Some kids wrapped a blanket on themselves underneath their dress. They were beaten and had to drop the blanket. We started to walk in those wooden shoes, clothed only in that one single dress. We walked and walked. I still remember the wind blowing, freezing; we walked for four or five days and nights. We never stopped. There was no shelter, no food. We were eating snow. I remember that. One by one I saw people dropping. These young people sat down—they couldn't walk anymore—and they froze to death. Either they were left there, or they were shot right in front of our eyes.

I was pulling my sister and yelling at the others not to sit down, not to stop, to keep walking. I was pulling my sister. I said, "You must help me, we have to stay together." I wanted to encourage her to hang on. And after maybe four or five days of walking, we came to a place in Germany called Gross-Rosen.[3] I don't have to tell you that most of the people didn't make it. I think about a thousand people left Hundsfeld and two hundred arrived at Gross-Rosen. The rest died on the road, frozen to death.

Interview #3

Saturday, July 3, 2004

This lingers in my mind that we walked for four or five days in bitter cold weather. We were followed by SS men on horseback and in cars. Of course, they didn't stay with us all the time; they rotated on different shifts. And we recognized that. I saw some of my friends, some of the girls just run away from the line. They probably froze on the side of the road; they just couldn't take it. But I had an attitude all the time—not to let the Nazis succeed. If I died, then they would have accomplished what they wanted.

I tried to encourage whomever I could not to sit down because once they sat down, they wouldn't get up. They would just freeze to death. Their blood would thicken and they would become extremely sleepy after a horrendous amount of exposure to the cold. I was pulling my sister; I remember pulling her just so she would not sit down. But secretly, I felt that maybe if I could fall down then I wouldn't have to walk anymore. But I didn't stay with that thought because I had a certain, not energy, but a will to survive so I could tell the world what was being done to us for no reason at all. I remember this feeling of emotional and physical exhaustion when we arrived at Gross-Rosen.

Was that in Germany?

Yes. Only about two hundred had survived, and the rest died. But we didn't stay here very long. The Nazis had us going back and forth to different concentration camps because lots of camps were being discovered. They grabbed whoever was still available to be gotten rid of and put as many people as they could on these death marches. You'll hear about it from other people too. It was meant for torture and to end it for us. That's why they were taking us from one place to another. We didn't stay at Gross-Rosen long, maybe about two days, no more than that. They gave us some black coffee or some hot liquid to drink and it was like heaven. Remember we had nothing to eat on the death walk; we just ate snow.

It gives me such a pain; I try not to think of these things in order to go on. I just can't even describe the agony, the pain, and the exposure to the weather, to the elements, and how horrible that was. As far as hunger goes, I suffered. My stomach was just shrinking. I was in pain for food. But somehow after a while, after a long while I got used to not eating; I just got weak. But water I never got used to not having. It was absent all the time. I'm trying to describe to you how bad it was. It is so difficult for me to talk about all this. I never really have, but I feel that I must do it now because there are books written that deny the Holocaust ever happened. This has to be from a sick mind, from a sick person, because there's lots of evidence that it did happen from those who are still alive and who survived. I gave you my tattoo number. That's something that a person just wouldn't do to herself.

Many years ago I wanted to remove the tattoo simply because I didn't want any sympathy. I didn't want to be looked at any differently from anyone else. I used to cover it up with makeup so people didn't ask me questions. I don't want the sympathy; I don't want to be different. And now that I have it, sometimes I think that maybe it's a good thing that I didn't remove it. Maybe it's good that I have it because with everything I went through, this is the proof that I need. Otherwise maybe I would think that I am nuts or I am imagining these things. Because it is so horrendous, it's easier to doubt it, especially if somebody makes it a business to write a book denying that anything happened. We are quite concerned that these deniers may succeed because it is hard to believe that people could do such things to each other. But they certainly did.

From Gross-Rosen, after a couple of days, the Germans packed us into transport wagons. These were not like the ones that took us to Auschwitz. Those were enclosed. These wagons had no top. They were like freight trains but with no top. And they ordered us in there; they packed us in real tight.

I neglected to tell you that I had another little cousin with me, a first cousin who was thirteen, the same age as my sister. She had stayed with us and with other relatives because her mother died during childbirth and her father couldn't take care of her. He also had two sons. And this little girl wound up like an orphan. So she stayed with me all during this time. She also tried to be brave, but it was very difficult. That memory just came into my mind just now, especially because after they packed us into these open-topped wagons, we sat down. There was enough room that you could pull up your leg and sit down. And don't forget that by then we were all so worn out. But she was climbing up on the open side of that wagon. She wanted to jump out. I remember that I held onto her leg and I held on to her dress and I was pulling her back. I begged her to just stay with me and we'd be fine. She was so distraught, she said to me, "I don't have to do this anymore. I don't have anybody to go home to; I am an orphan. I don't have a mom." And she wanted to end it right then so she didn't have to suffer. Of course I didn't let her jump out.

Again we were riding on this open freight train; don't forget this was January 1945, and this journey took several days. We went through towns and farms; I remember some farmers threw some vegetables to us—radishes and other things. We grabbed them. We even shared because we had no food, no sanitation, and no water. I don't even know how I did it. After several days, which seemed like a long time, maybe it was close to a week that we had been driving and stopping and driving and stopping. Don't forget these were freight trains; they didn't travel like regular trains. They brought us again into an overnight stop called Mauthausen.[4] That was a men's camp; mostly men were brought there. And I saw men like zombies walking around aimlessly—muselman.[5] Nobody was normal; everybody was in another state; we weren't functioning human beings. But here too they unloaded us and we stayed overnight. Again they were trying to elude the Allies so they wouldn't know where we were. The next day we were packed into the same open transportation cars. And again we began traveling. I think we were traveling for about thirteen days. All of the sudden it dawned on me that I hadn't eaten anything. As I said before, I just didn't think about it anymore because I never saw myself in a mirror. But I looked down at my leg and my arm and they were like sticks.

After about thirteen days of zigzagging they brought us to the most horrible camp called Bergen-Belsen in Germany.[6] I couldn't believe what I was seeing. They put us in barracks. They had no windows but they had doors. There was nothing to lie on, just a bare floor. There was no blanket, there was no bed, there was no mattress, there was nothing. Here they didn't have to count us anymore. There was no water, and I remember some people couldn't manage anymore without water; they drank their own urine out of a bowl. And I remember if it rained, we ran outside and just tried to drink whatever the ground didn't soak up.

By that time my sister was very weak. I used to go outside just to see what was happening. The people here were zombies. There were dead people all over outside; they were just lying on the ground. And then the bodies were piled up, like a farmer piles up what he harvests. The bodies were just thrown on top of each other; a mountain of bodies was spread out every which way. There was an arm here, a leg there, a head somewhere else. This was so devastating to see that after a while I didn't want to go outside anymore.

My sister was very sick; she had diarrhea. They had some sort of a trench that they dug nearby to go to if we wanted to relieve ourselves. People just kind of squatted and aimed for the hole. There was no sanitation whatsoever to wash our hands or anything. A lot of people died from typhus. I was there for about three months, from the end of January until April 19, 1945, just diminishing and disappearing. My legs looked even thinner. There was just bone. My arms were just bones. And then I couldn't walk; my knees wouldn't hold me up anymore. If I fell down on the ground, I would have no way of getting up.

My sister, also very sick, became very quiet. I still kept telling her to hang on because we would be okay, and we would have to go home. It was always that same story to try to keep her alive. I think we got some black coffee in the beginning, but after a while we got nothing. People were walking outside to find anything that was edible. No matter what it was, they would pick it up. I was so weak that I no longer could walk. But of course I stayed in this place; as I said we had arrived at the end of January, and were there through February, March, and to the end of April. So it was nearly three months of this kind of a suffering. Everyday I saw the Germans come in the barracks and whoever was not moving they grabbed, either by the hair, an arm, or a leg, and they pulled them outside and threw them on the pile.

I also remember that I befriended a couple of ladies who were much older than my sister and I. And they were kind; you know they tried to talk to us a little bit. I don't remember anything real specific, but there were some people that were talking to us.

One day, I started to break out all over on my body. It was like scabs, like wounds, breaking out all over my whole body and in my hair. And in that flesh, that infected flesh were living lice. They were all over, in our clothes, on the dresses we wore, in the seams. We were covered, wherever we looked. They were a whitish color, gray lice. By the millions. We were covered with them. They were in my head and all over my body living in those infections. And the infection started to get in my mouth; I couldn't open my mouth anymore. I couldn't lift my arm; I was covered with them. And one day, even though I couldn't hear well, I heard that something was going on outside. This was already into April. And I crawled outside because I always wanted to know in my head what was going on. I crawled outside and looked up and the sky was covered with airplanes, hundreds of airplanes circling us. They came low and it was very noisy. Somehow I felt that we were being discovered, which really did happen. So I crawled back into the barrack and—this is very hard for me to tell. I took my sister and somehow I pulled her real close to me; I was holding her in my arms. And she couldn't hold up her head anymore. It just fell on her chest. It just hung down, but she was alive. I said to her, "Listen Ebey, there are airplanes out there, we are being discovered. In no time we will be taken back home to our families. Just don't get down, stay strong and concentrate on that." And while I was telling her she died in my arms. Then somebody came and pulled her out and that was the end of me. I knew she was in the pile. My little cousin, also named Ibolya, had died too, a couple of days before. She also had been thrown on the pile. I was all by myself.

That night soldiers came running back into the barracks. They were talking to us; I spoke a little bit of German at that time. They spoke to us in languages that we could understand. And they were telling us that they were our friends, and they were there to help us. I still remember one soldier had opened a can of beans and he was putting it in my mouth so that I ate it. He thought that if I ate something I would instantly be better, but that nearly killed me. I was so sick. I still remember the pain, the cold beans. They were putting crackers in people's mouths. They just wanted to feed us because we were starving.

What happened after the soldiers came and tried to put food in your mouth?

That was very destructive. We hadn't eaten for so long, so it was very painful. But they set up emergency hospitals, and they began taking people out. They told us they were going to take us to the hospital. They'd have food for us, and they would get us cleaned up. They were saying all these encouraging things, and I remember I was lying there and I said to myself, they are not going to take me because I am not worth it; I am almost not even alive anymore. I imagined that they would take the others, but they were not going to take me. But I didn't care by then; I didn't care; it didn't matter. I think because I lost my sister and my cousin, I couldn't encourage myself anymore. It just didn't matter. I accepted that. But they did take me. It must have been in an ambulance because I remember I was on a stretcher in a car. And so they set up these emergency hospitals, and they took me to one nearby.

Once there they put me in bed and then two nurses put me into a tub filled with hot water. I couldn't hear then and I couldn't speak either. Whatever they did to me they did. But I remember sitting in this tub and one nurse was holding both of my hands. The other one was using a big scrubbing floor brush, as if she had a very soiled floor and she needed to scrub it. And while I was sitting in this water she was pulling off all of the scabs, all those wounds that I had, and was cleaning them out with that brush. She had to because as I said there were lice living in them. I was screaming; I remember I was crying. And that nurse that was holding my hand was crying very much too, with tears. She tried to soothe me but she was also crying. And then after this torture was over, they covered me. They put me in bed and covered me completely with a yellow medicine. I guess that was to prevent the infections from coming back, I don't know.

I was in this hospital until the beginning of July 1945. While I was in the hospital the doctors would come to examine me. I was in bed with a blanket. I would not let go of that blanket. I didn't trust people because I didn't know who they were. And I remember that they motioned to each other to just let it go and not to force me. This went on for a while; I don't really remember that much or being alert at all. I remember having nightmares, seeing my family, talking to my father and my brother. I think I must have had a very high fever. I was always very cold, bitter cold. It didn't matter what they covered me with. I was just so cold. My spirit was totally gone. It's almost as if I was just out of order. I just couldn't handle it anymore; I was detached from myself. I remember the nightmares. They tried to give me food, and I wouldn't eat it; I couldn't eat it, I just didn't want it. And I remember then somebody came; a doctor was telling us that we needed special nourishment; we needed special care that they could not give us there. Europe was war torn. He said we would go to either Switzerland or Sweden so we could get the proper care to recover.

This first hospital was in Germany?

Yes, this was in Germany. And I remember I was communicating somehow to whoever was giving us this information that I was not interested. I was not going to Switzerland or Sweden. And yet he was talking about food, about eggs, milk, and bread. And I said to myself, "Oh yeah, there is such a thing, I used to know that. There is such a thing as milk." I had already blocked all that out completely. But I said I was not going because I was going back to Hungary to be with my family. And I promised myself that I had survived so we would all be together again. And then the man said to everybody that if we thought we were going to go home, where we came from, there was no such a thing. "You don't have any home or any place else." He told us our parents were most likely gone and that we shouldn't think about going back. We should just go with this new idea.

I remember I was broken-hearted when he told me that whatever I had thought of surviving for, there was no such a thing. It was horrendous. So I didn't fight it anymore. They put tags around our neck, a little disc with a number, and they brought us to a port. We were all lined up, lots of us on stretchers. And they left us on the ground until they could transport us. I also remember that on the way to this port (I don't know the name of the port; half the time I was in and out of consciousness); they took me on a warm water mattress on some sort of a train because I had no meat on me. My back had a sore from being beaten, and it never healed, as a result of the malnutrition. My friends used to tell me that they could see my intestines. I still have a scar on my back that's about two inches wide from that beating. It healed over but it's very sensitive skin. If I wear something tight, it's very painful. So they put me on this hot water mattress. And they must have given me a drug, possibly morphine. This was to make me feel as if I could make it. From the train they put me on a stretcher and we were lined up and transported to a ship. I was told that we were going to a foreign country. I was wondering how I would know where I was. And how would I know when I got there? We arrived at a city named Kalmar in Sweden.

Do you know about when this was?

July 1945. It was the first week in July and I still wasn't myself. I wasn't coping with anything anymore; I was just alive. They emptied the hospitals in Sweden to accommodate the survivors. I cannot tell you enough how the Swedish people were concerned and kind and tireless. Every Swede volunteered in that hospital, even the unskilled. They were peeling vegetables, they were cooking, and they were cleaning. Every Swede volunteered. I still wondered how I would know where I was. And then they gave us breakfast, it must have been like oatmeal, something I never ate before. And I said to myself, oh now I am probably in this foreign country because the food is different. The nurses would feed me even if I didn't want to eat. I cannot tell you how good they were to me. By now I weighed 54 pounds; I was nineteen years old, and I was like a bag of bones.

I remember the doctor would come by the bed and he would tell me in Swedish that I must eat a lot. But my appetite wasn't there. Still, the nurses came in the middle of the night and asked if I wanted to eat something. And they would make it. They would just go in the kitchen and make something for me. They were tap dancing for me, holding onto the bed and tap dancing for me. My hair was growing back and they would comb my hair. And they would soothe me and would do anything to make me feel better. They were very kind. I had to stay in this hospital for a whole year. They taught me how to walk again, as you do with babies.

One held me and the other one held out a hand so I could take a few steps to get to her. Then after a few months they taught me to hold onto a railing and walk slowly. And after I was able to do that then I went to the bathroom. The bathroom was in the hall, not in the room. And I sat down on the toilet and I looked down at my legs and they were like sticks, there was no meat on them. That's when I realized what a condition I was in because I had not seen a mirror for a long time. I'll never forget that; I realized that it wasn't like me. And then I looked at my arm and it was the same thing. I looked like a skeleton.

I still remember that so clearly, how I was strong all through the year, but in the last three months in Bergen-Belsen from where I was liberated, I really lost all my flesh. I lost all my humanity, everything. That was a very hard part of my life, and it's very hard for me to talk about. I try to protect myself as I am talking to you and not get too emotional because it hurts, and I can't handle it. I have a pain in my throat right now.

Eventually my appetite started coming back. I know that because when I heard noises in the kitchen, like dishes knocking together, I would look forward to the food coming. I remember this. After a whole year, the nurses wanted to take me to a concert. They bought the tickets and showed me that they were going to take me to a concert. Remember, I hadn't been outside in the open air for months. I tried but I couldn't go. I asked them to put me back in bed. I just couldn't do it. My memory of this is excellent because they were kind and we were friends. After a year with a caretaker I was put into a convalescent home, a place that you go when you don't need the hospital anymore, but you still can't live on your own. I was scared but I was also looking forward to a change.

I had befriended a girl in the hospital. Her name was Susan. Maybe that's why I named your mom Susan. She was from Budapest. We became good friends. She was sick also. But she had a mother in Budapest who had survived; I think she was in hiding so they couldn't take her. And she wrote to her mother and said that she has a sister and asked if she could bring me to her. When she was going back, she would take me with her, and her mom would also be my mom. That was very touching. The communication was not easy because there was no mail or any kind of communication between Hungary and Sweden; everything was destroyed during the war; however, if you knew somebody in Czechoslovakia, you could send a letter there and from there they could send it to Budapest. That's how Susan used to write. And her mother said I could come with her. It was very comforting, but, at the same time, I didn't want to go back to Hungary. We were also together in the convalescent home. By then, somehow I was able to write. We were encouraged to write to an organization—I think it was the Hebrew Immigrant Aid Society (HIAS)—to look for any siblings or anybody left in our families that may have survived.

HIAS also had some volunteers that visited us. I remember they gave me a prayer book. And I still have that. That's what I wrote in, while I could still think. I wrote down my parents' birthdays and also my siblings' birthdays so I wouldn't forget them. So we were put into this convalescent home. And we got our meals there, but we didn't do anything, just took it easy while we recovered. Still we made friends; we slept in barracks with lots of bunk beds. I was in this convalescent home for another year before I was able to leave. I wrote to the HIAS, and I filled out a form to look for all of my siblings. They wrote back. It took months, but a telegram came to me saying that I had a brother. They didn't know where he was, but they knew he was alive. This was known from the bookkeeping of the Germans. They registered everything. When I got the telegram, I was hysterical. They had to sit on me; I was just going nuts. I had a brother! I had already given up on everybody. And now, through my friend Susan, I wrote to Czechoslovakia. I just kept on writing. I didn't know which brother was alive, but I kept writing to my hometown. He was getting the letters, but he could never write back because he had no way of knowing how to go about getting letters back to me. Somehow I found out which brother was there—Miklos. I was elated.

In the meantime I also inquired whether anyone knew anything about my mother or father. I knew about my mother because we were told that mothers were put in the gas chambers with their young children. I wondered about my father. One day I got a telegram saying that Martin Blum was alive in Russia. That was my father's name. But his birthday didn't match my father's. The telegram asked if I was sure about my father's birthday. I was sure. When that telegram came, I was so hysterical. I didn't speak English, but in the print his name was written, and I thought that they were telling me that he was alive. I just went nuts. I even tore the telegram. I still have it you know.

Unfortunately, however, it was somebody else. Later on with the help of searchers, they were able to tell me exactly what happened to my mother and my younger siblings. They were all put in the gas chamber at Auschwitz on the same day in June 1944, the day we arrived. They then told me where my father died and where my older brother died.   They died in Mauthausen (in the male camp) from exposure and malnutrition. My father died on December 14, 1944; my older brother, Sandor, on March 19, 1945. I have the dates because they were able to track them down.

Interview #4

Saturday, August 21, 2004

What was the convalescent home like?

They were wooden buildings, like barracks. They had beds; it was almost like a dormitory, but I don't recall that much about it. That's how we were accommodated. There was a woman in the house who was in charge of us because we all were teenagers. And Sweden was wonderful, I mean they really gave us a chance, or gave me a chance to become human again. When I had first arrived to Sweden I was a goner. I weighed 54 pounds. I was a bag of bones. I was terribly malnourished. So I stayed in Sweden after the convalescent home.

How did you decide specifically where you would go after the hospital?

The people from the convalescent home suggested that I join a group of girls in the city of Jönköping in Sweden. They were renting a house and I would be one of the tenants. I would live on my own, but with other girls. We went to work; I was taught how to use a sewing machine. Two girls stayed home to cook and clean. There were thirteen of us. Eleven went to work so we could pay the rent and get food. With the money that we all made, we put everything together; we didn't have anything separate.

While I was in that home we were written up in the newspaper because our culture was not the same as the Scandinavian countries and Sweden. The boys and girls there were about free love and no marriage and babies, and we, the thirteen of us, were not. That just wasn't our lifestyle. We were written about in the newspaper on the front pages. It said that we live on this street in this house and we don't go with boys. We were like freaks. People looked at us like, who are you? But other than that, for the most part, people were honest and loving.

There's no stealing in Sweden, at least at that time. I'm sure it has changed since the Second World War. But if you bought something in a store and you forgot to take it with you, or if you were reading a book and you left it in the park, nobody would take it. And you could go back the next day, and you'd still find it where you left it, unmoved. Their philosophy was that it is not yours, why would you take it? If somebody took something that wasn't theirs, they would be considered mentally sick because they took someone else's thing that didn't belong to them.

Yes. It's amazing. I left a suitcase one time. I was traveling on a train, and I heard that I could leave my suitcase there; I didn't have to take it with me. And back then the suitcases didn't have wheels! I asked inside where they sell the tickets, "Can I leave my suitcase here? I'll be gone for a while." A woman said, "Yes, you can." Then I asked, "Will it be there when I come back?" The woman said, "Well, who would take it? It's yours."

As I was working, I learned the language very quickly. And then I was thinking about maybe living in Israel. Some of my friends were already leaving to go there. At that time it was Palestine; there was no Israel yet. Maybe it just became Israel, the new country. Of course, I wasn't strong enough to even think about actually doing that yet. But I was thinking about where I would end up. I knew I didn't want to remain in Sweden because that lifestyle just wasn't for me. I was very lonesome. I remember how I used to feel—almost frightened, you know, full of anxiety. I had been pushed around so much in my young life that I was concerned very much about where I'd wind up. I had no one in America as far as I knew.

I was able to correspond by then, not often, but somehow with my brother who went back to Hungary. My brother Miklos had walked back to Hungary after he was freed from the last concentration camp he was in. He wrote to me and asked me to come back to Hungary as well. But I had no desire to go back. Our house was empty—my family wasn't there; it just wasn't the same. Hungary had a Communist government, so I knew if I went back I wouldn't be able to get out again. I told my brother through letters to get out of Hungary and go to a displaced persons camp to get help. I could then meet him in the new country, Israel. This was my plan. Miklos was able to pay somebody to smuggle him out of the country in a refrigerator box. He ended up in Germany where he went to a displaced persons organization that put him into school.

One time my brother wrote me a letter and sent me an address saying that the people at that address were related to us. The address was my father's aunt. She and her family went to America before the Second World War, in the early thirties. And my brother said in his letter that there were some children there and they were related. If I wanted to write to them that would be okay. So I did. I was hoping that maybe they would answer me. And that's exactly what I wrote to them, that I was just writing to them to let them know who I was and that I had survived. I said I would just like to know that I have somebody in this world, some family, some relatives somewhere. I asked if they would be kind enough to answer me. And they did. My father's aunt was already about eighty years or older, and she gave my letter to her daughter. And I remember she sent me two dollars, two single American dollars in the letter. I felt so rich. I had two American dollars.

She wrote in Hungarian and I was very pleased. And then I wrote to them again thanking them for the money and then a second letter came. She asked me if I would like to come to America. You can imagine how I felt. You can imagine my feelings, my hopes, and my dreams that maybe, just maybe, it would come true. I wrote back and I told them how grateful I would be and that I would never cost them any money because I knew how to sew. I could rent a room if only they could just help me come there. That's another long story but they did help me.

I arrived in America on June 14, 1948. Coming to America was a dream, an unbelievable dream. But my father's cousin, whom I came to live with, was hoping that I was a signal from her oldest son, a United States pilot and a veterinarian, who had disappeared while on a mission. His plane was shot down and lost over Belgium. And his mother (I called her Tanta [Aunt] Malvina) was really my father's cousin but I called her Tanta, could not accept that. She thought that I was a sign from her son. She couldn't accept what happened.

That he died?
Yes. She had a nervous breakdown. Through therapy treatments she was somehow made to believe that he probably had amnesia somewhere because they never got a notice about him. Because I was all alone and out of the blue I wrote her this letter, she thought that it was a signal to them that their son would write next. She thought he would no longer have amnesia and he would come back. They worked with Beth Jacob Seminary for Girls in Williamsburg, New York, that sponsored me so I could go to school. They were supposed to give me room and board and they did. I lived with them for close to a year.

With the school or with the family?
With Tanta and her husband. They had three sons, who were already married. But the letter never came from their son. Soon they realized that I wasn't a signal so they moved to Israel and left me on the street.

Really? How long were you in America by then?
Close to a year. She got me a job in a factory where I made about twenty dollars a week. I wasn't supposed to, or even allowed to be working, but I'm telling you how it was because these are the facts.

I wasn't allowed to work because I was a student. When she told me they were leaving, they didn't prepare me for anything. I was literally on the street. I had two girlfriends, two sisters—Toby and Sarah Berkowitz—who were not far from where I lived. I went over to them and asked if I could live with them. They checked with the landlady who was renting them a room. She said no. She didn't want any more tenants. The next day

Tanta was leaving with her husband for Israel. I was walking with my friend. Her name is Sarah. We were walking up and down the street because sometimes these homes in Brooklyn, New York, rent out rooms.

This was in Brooklyn?

Yes, Brooklyn. And there was a sign in a window that said "Room to Let." We could hardly see it because it was already getting dark, but we went in there and I asked them if it was still available and they said yes. I said I'd be over the next day and I would bring my stuff. I didn't even ask about a kitchen or anything; I was just so glad that there was a room where I could stay. I think they wanted twenty dollars for rent. I gave them a deposit, but nothing was officially done. I came the next day with my one suitcase because I didn't own much else. And when I got there they wanted to know my name. I gave them my name and it turned out that we had the same last name.

Really?

Just by chance. My name was Blum and so was theirs. Well they got so excited, and the man insisted that I was a niece and was related to him. And I said, "Mr. Blum, even my grandfather was born in Hungary." At that time he was 62 years old. To me he was like a real old man.

And he said, "Lizbet," they called me, "Lizbet." He said he had a brother that ran away from the family when he was twelve years old. He probably wound up in Hungary, so we were related. I tell you, they treated me so well. They didn't treat their own child better. They were like my parents.

Then they asked me how I was going to eat. I had never even thought about that. I said that I could always get bread and make a sandwich. They said, "No, no, no, you will eat with us." And they made me dinner. The dinner was either twenty-five cents or thirty-five cents. They were so good to me. There was dinner when I came home from school or from work. The only trouble was that for about three months I ate the same thing every single night for dinner. It was soup with a piece of beef in it, every single night. And after three months I just couldn't eat it anymore. I told her that it was very good but I just couldn't eat it anymore. She was so surprised she said, "Lizbet, just tell me what you want, I'll make it for you." So I said liver or a piece of chicken. And she would make it for me for the same money. I'm sure she paid more for it in the store. They were so good to me, I cannot tell you enough.

I had a lot of trouble with my teeth. I would go to a clinic in New York because I had no money. At this place they would take anyone because they were learning on us. Sometimes I was late for dinner because I had to take the subway, and Mr. Blum would be furious at me because they were worried about where I was. They said I must call if I couldn't be home on time, or if I was running late because they worried about me.

How do you feel about Hungary today?

Well, I'm really at home in America. This is where I am at home. And as far as how I feel, I think I just have to look back at what I have done or haven't done since I came to America. I never had the desire to go back to Hungary. That should tell you a lot. No. No. No. And for me that was a long time ago, and I just put it aside. I am interested if I hear about the country on the news or if I read about it. I am interested, but as far as going back goes, I am surprised that anyone went back. But they did, because otherwise they'd have to learn a different language and adjust to a different lifestyle. But I am glad I was able to come to America. I love the United States. There is no place like it, no place in the whole wide world. Even though we have faults, it is still the best place in the whole world. I only wish I grew up here because I was a good student. I was very interested in doing something with my life. But I was just born at the wrong time, and I never had a real opportunity.

When you first came to America did anyone ask you about your experiences?

No.

About everything that happened? Nobody said anything?

Nobody talked about it for a long time.

When did you start talking about everything that happened?

Well, actually I didn't. I didn't even tell your mom or Kenny, my son, about the horrors that I went through because I didn't want to make them sad. I just tried to be strong and healthy, both physically and mentally, and raise them like normal. I didn't say anything. It took many years, ten or fifteen years at least, when finally there were leaders here in the United States that felt that it had to be dealt with. This is how people slowly came forward, and it all was recorded. A few years ago Steven Spielberg wanted to document everybody's life that survived the Holocaust. And they came to the house to interview me, but I couldn't do it. I still couldn't do it.

One time I made an appointment with King's College. That was the first place I think where they advertised in the paper for Holocaust survivors to come forward. They wanted to interview us. I remember your dad gave this article to your mom to send to me when I lived up in Park Ridge, New Jersey, and she sent it to me. I read it and I thought that if your father feels that this is something I should look into, then I must do it. I called the college and made an appointment. Then they told me that it would be recorded. I thought I was just going to talk to somebody, but they said there would be a camera and they would record it. I just couldn't do it, so I cancelled the appointment. I find it very difficult to talk to you too because I don't want to make you sad you know? And yet I do the best I can, but it's very hard, it's very hard on me.

Is it important to you to share your story?

Well, not to me. It's not that I feel that I must share my story, but I feel that it should be known. And, therefore, if I am asked to talk, I do. I went to schools a few times and talked to the children, and I can see that my story makes an impression on them. The last time I went to the Holocaust Museum in Cherry Hill, a nice gentleman who was in charge introduced me. And he told the children that I was there so they could meet me, not for sympathy, but so they could better understand that part of history. I found myself trying to protect myself and them at the same time. They heard me and paid attention, and the response I got was unbelievable. Unbelievable. These children, all of them came up to me, boys and girls came up and hugged me and gave me a kiss. They were not just shaking my hand.

I was so touched. But I was so beat up from my own story that it took me a few days to be myself again. So I don't do it that much anymore because it's just too difficult for me. Your question was, is it important? Just as I told the children, it's important to not always be followers. They should question when they see and hear things that don't sit right with them. They should have their own input and judgment because there are a lot of enemies out there for different reasons and for different ethnic groups. But the reaction of the children is wonderful. They send me notes, they were really moved by my story, and for that reason it is important. But, for me personally, no, I don't feel better.

What happened the first time you saw your brother Miklos? How long had it been and what was it like?

Thirty-one years. I really had such a hard life. It's hard to believe that a person could go through all this. By the time I saw him, he had changed so much. I wasn't able to visit him in Israel before that because your original grandfather, my first husband, wouldn't go; he could care less. But when your Papa and I got married, he felt that it was time to see my brother. This meeting was something else. We couldn't even talk to each other; we just kept repeating each other's names and crying. It felt like the vein in my neck was just burning and it was going to explode. And his kids were pulling on us. He had little children and older ones. They all wanted to know why we were crying. They didn't know what had happened. And it was touching. When I went back the second time, then we could really visit.

How do you feel about Germany today? Do you have any hatred or any kind of feelings as a result of what happened?

No, I don't have any hatred. I feel that they really broke many lives; most of them are not here anymore. I feel that maybe they are trying to do the right thing today. Seeing those kids that were at your house, those German exchange high school children, and the concert/play they put on, made me see that Germany is different today. When I went to that concert I felt very down. I really didn't want to see a German concert because I didn't know what it was about. I couldn't help but have very great doubts about what I was going to hear or see. But when the concert started, those young children put on that play about Marlene Dietrich, who was known for being very much against the Nazis, not only in her head but in her actions as well. She did many things to show her dislike and distrust for them.[7]

That play was very impressive, and it showed how the Germans now are teaching this to the younger children. Everything was in English, so we could understand it, and I must tell you that I came away with such a light heart to see that they are coping with their history. They need to because what they did to the world is beyond explanation and for no reason at all. Hitler spoke very loud, very strong, and he was very sure of himself.

People did not question what or whom they were following; they just followed. And this is why I tell the young children to listen and think for themselves. Don't become followers.

But still I would never want to go to Germany because if I had money to spend, I'd spend it here in the United States. There is plenty to see here and I'm home, I'm secure, and I'm unafraid. And I haven't seen enough of the USA.

Do you think it's possible for something like the Holocaust to happen again?

Everything has to be watched very carefully because it can happen again. Maybe not exactly the same way, but it can happen. The world is very dangerous today. I feel very sad that the young people like you have such a world that's so dangerous and so unpredictable. It's awful. Everybody should live and let live. You don't have to love people, but you at least have to respect people, and that's not always happening.

It's very scary, but I don't feel bad for myself anymore; I lived my life, and I had my share. But I always feel very bad for my grandchildren and everybody's grandchildren. Families are so important. Love each other; take care of each other because family is the best thing in the world and that's the only thing that's for sure today. I never really had that because I lost everybody at such an early age. Sometimes I look at myself as a "mystery person." Where did I come from? What happened to me? That's why when your mom was born, oh my God. I had my own child. I wrote her a message on her birthday card when she was fifty years old. Ask her to show it to you.

I wrote to her about when she was little. I remember it as if it were yesterday. It was like a miracle, this little bundle. She's my own flesh and blood. I used to talk to her all the time. Some of my neighbors were outside laughing; they thought I had a friend in my house. But I would talk to her all the time telling her what we were going to do next, what she was going to wear, and who we were going to meet outside. I just talked to her all the time.

Have you told Kenny or mom much about your experiences? Have you ever really sat down and talked about it? Or do they just know bits and pieces?

No. I didn't. I don't know if you want to go into this, but your grandfather, their father, my first husband, was not a good man. He was only interested in himself, his food, his comfort, his needs, and that's it. So he never asked anything; he never wanted to know. We never had a conversation about it. He was just a cruel man. I was stuck because I had nobody to turn to. And as long as we did not discuss anything I could not possibly tell my daughter or my son about everything and then just go on about my life. He was so horrible as a father, aside from being horrible to me, that I wanted to make sure that your mom and Uncle Kenny had at least one sane person, so to speak, so they would not be warped.

I wanted to be a good example to them. I never fought with their father. He was awful. I was like a slave, and I was just waiting for some day to end it. It was another concentration camp for me until I freed myself. In the meantime, I had no other place to bring my kids. Sometimes I thought I would just go to the park and sit there and see what happens, but I would never leave my children. Still, it was a miserable, miserable sixteen years. And when they were old enough, I went to school. I was already in my early forties. I knew that I could somehow earn a living. I also knew that I could not count on him. So I went to school. I went to learn to be a hair stylist. And I was there always learning and practicing, and I got my license a year later. I went to school for a year and when I got my license, I went to see a lawyer and I got a divorce. Your mom and Uncle Kenny were with me. They were happy. I always told them what was happening. They knew I was going to do something about the situation, but it had to be timed right so everybody would be okay, including him. I never talked badly of him; he did that himself. But as soon as I got my first paycheck, I knew that I could make it.

Do you think part of the reason you wanted to become a hair stylist is because you did people's hair in the concentration camp?

Yes, definitely. Definitely. I went to school while we were married. I went to secretarial school. At that time I had to learn to type and take shorthand and the machines weren't modern yet. He tore up my books. I couldn't go to work because he was very possessive. He would ask, "How will my dinner be hot when I come home if you are working?   How will you walk the dog if you are working?" He found all sorts of excuses as to why I couldn't work. He wouldn't let me because he was just a horrible person. If he weren't afraid of the law, he probably would have locked me in the house so I couldn't get out. It's hard to believe. And I am telling you mildly how awful it was.

Are there any of your experiences during the Holocaust that you think most people don't really know about? A lot of research has been done, but is there anything that sticks out in your mind that maybe people don't know as much about that they should know? Is there anything else you want to explain?

Well, there were many concentration camps. And everybody's experiences are different. No matter how much you hear about it, you cannot possibly register how horrendous it was for me and for so many others. We had no food; we had nothing—yesterday, today, or tomorrow. There were times when I had no food for two weeks, nothing. Nothing. Eventually I may have had some hot broth liquid with some grass in it, but there weren't any recognizable vegetables. That hunger starved my brain and me at the same time, I became like a zombie. And water. There was no water. I'm not even talking about having a shower or washing my face. I'm talking about drinking water. There was none, none. There were no other liquids either, none. Then there was the cold, so extreme that even today I think I would rather go hungry than be cold the way I was then. We stood in line. There was no heat, not even in the barracks, but at least we were indoors. And then we would stand outside for hours. I had no coat; I didn't even have underwear. I just had that one dress. We were so cold that we just huddled together when they were not looking so our body heat would somehow generate a little warmth.

It was such torture, such suffering; it's hard to believe. I don't blame people that question how this could be possible. There are some nuts that write books saying that it never happened. Some people will believe that because it was so awful that it's easier to think that people couldn't possibly withstand it. But of course, that's why six million Jews died, and millions of others too. Most people died. Only the young and the strong remained. How I made it I don't know. I'm sure a lot had to do with my sister being with me and trying to stay strong for her, to show her that we could do it. That had something to do with it, but in the end she didn't make it.

But that says a lot about you. That you did make it and so many others didn't. Sometimes, when I am determined to do something and I actually do it, I think some of the qualities that you have rubbed off on me.

I often thought that maybe I would be better off dying with

the rest of them. I'd just be finished. But you can't talk like that. It's not up to me.

Think of how successful my mom is and how well we're doing. None of that would have been.

She is such a whole person. That's right; this is what I told you. And I see your mother so many times, strong, as I used to be. I don't have that anymore. I used to think that nothing was too much. I always had a tomorrow on my mind. And there was a reason for what I did and why I did it. I remember when she was about four or five years old, we moved to Ridgefield, New Jersey. She would say to me all the time, "Mommy, I want to be just like you when I grow up." She said this as a little girl. Do you know how pleased I was?

Yes, I'm sure you were. We all turned out well and it's a good thing that you were so strong and determined. You stood up for what was right and now look at everything that has happened because of that. It's pretty good.

Postscript

In 1950, my grandmother married her first husband. They had two children, Susan and Kenny. Years later she divorced this man and became a hairdresser. She eventually met Samuel Goldstein, whom she married in 1973. She was happily married to Samuel until he passed away in September 1995. Today, my grandmother resides in Mount Laurel, New Jersey, close to family and friends. She enjoys the company of her cat, Kitty, as well as playing bridge and spending time with loved ones.

As I watched the tears well up in my grandmother's eyes throughout the process of interviewing her, I couldn't help but open my heart to her. As I stared at the faded tattoo permanently engraved into her arm, a constant reminder of her horrific past, I couldn't even begin to relate to the experiences she has been through.

I cannot fathom what life must have been like for her. Imagine being ridiculed and humiliated on a daily basis by the people you used to know as friends. Imagine being taken from your home in Hungary at the young age of eighteen, not knowing where you were going or what was happening to you and your family. Imagine being taken to a ghetto to live in a small attic with five other families for weeks. Then she was deported to Auschwitz in a small cattle car, packed in so tightly that people became mentally unstable. There was no food or water, just fear all around. I cannot imagine arriving in Auschwitz and watching people shot right before my eyes. My grandmother didn't realize that she would never see most of her family again, as they would be killed in a matter of hours. Time rolled by as she watched her body starve, with the stench of death invading all that she did. Then, transported with her sister to Plaszow, near Krakow in Poland, they worked in extreme heat for months. They were beaten and tortured on a regular basis. Then she was brought back to Auschwitz in Poland, where a tattoo on her arm would be a physical scar reminding her for the rest of her life of all she had endured. Most other prisoners' lives were very short-lived. The tattoos took away their identities and dehumanized them. They no longer were people, just meaningless numbers. I cannot imagine standing in line for hours, naked, being inspected for blemishes, birthmarks, and imperfections. The punishment for having these imperfections was death.

After a month at Auschwitz, she was taken to Hundsfeld, Germany, where she had to work in an ammunition factory making the very same bullets that could potentially kill her or her sister. She was severely beaten for sabotaging the production of this ammunition. Then, after three months in the bitter cold, she was forced to leave the concentration camp and walk on a journey designed to exhaust the prisoners until they died. Walking for four to five days in the extreme cold with nothing to eat but snow, she continued to push on. She arrived at Gross-Rosen, another concentration camp in Germany, spending the night still fighting to stay alive.

The next day she was taken in subzero temperatures on an open-topped train to Mauthausen, Austria, yet another camp where she would suffer. Barely alive, she was then taken to Bergen-Belsen, a concentration camp in Germany. There she fought death on an hourly basis. Her sister, Ibolya, was her sole motivation to survive. After three agonizing months, she finally got a sign of hope for survival, but at the same time, her worst nightmare came true. Her sister died in her arms just as the soldiers came in to liberate them. How she was able to experience all that and still find the will to hold on is beyond me.

We have it so good in America. We take far too much for granted. My grandmother has experienced such a hard life and has still somehow managed to be positive, encouraging, and enthusiastic. I feel bad that she has suffered so much, and it bothers me to know that every time we discuss her past, it brings all those painful memories rushing back. It takes her days to recover. I come home a changed person every time I leave her house, and I appreciate her so much. It's indescribable. She has survived one of the most devastating events in history.

For an entire year she was tortured while she watched people slowly die and decay both physically and mentally all around her. How she survived that is beyond me, but I know that it wasn't her time to die. She was meant to be on this earth for a long time. She impacts the lives of everyone she meets in a positive way. She has accomplished so much with the few opportunities she has been given. She could have chosen to give up on life many times, but instead she decided to stay strong and fight for what she believed. Those actions are so admirable that they have made me want to share her story and make a difference. The world is a better place because of her. If one person treats another with a little kindness because of her, if one person isn't so judgmental because of her experiences, and if one person can accept others' differences and respect them instead of fighting because of her, then my goal in sharing her story has been achieved.

I owe my life to her stubbornness and her will to survive, and for that I cannot repay her enough. I am so grateful that she never gave up, and sometimes I feel as though I can do anything because she has proven that everything is possible. I owe it to her to tell people her story and to make them understand the importance of recognizing that when something isn't right, you have to stand up for what you believe in.

There are too many times that I hear people stereotype a group of people in a negative way and judge them by the way they look or something about them. It's not right. I hope that as a result of this book, some people will see the devastating effects that those judgments and stereotypes can have. More than six million Jewish people were killed in the Holocaust—a devastating number. They were killed not because they did anything wrong, but simply because of who they were.

Questions about God, religion, and what it means to be a human being inevitably surface when one studies the Holocaust and other genocides. That people had to experience "hell on earth" forces me to ponder a few questions. Where was God? Where were human beings? Why did people kill other people? These are only a few of the questions I often ask myself. What I have come to realize through my study of the Holocaust is that I have a duty to learn from them about what they went through and an obligation to see to it, insofar as I can, that such things do not happen again.

I am grateful to my grandmother. She told me her story in the hope that as people are educated, they will learn more compassion. Those who make an effort to be a little more open and understanding carry the hope of a peaceful future. Please pass on that hope to others.

"First, they came for the communists,
and I did not speak up
because I was not a communist;

Then, they came for the socialists,
and I did not speak up
because I was not a socialist;

They came for the union leaders (Gewerkschaftler),
and I did not speak up
because I wasn't a union leader;

They came for the Jews,
and I did not speak up
because I wasn't a Jew;

Then they came for me,
and there was no one left
to speak up for me."

—Pastor Martin Niemoller, 1946[8]

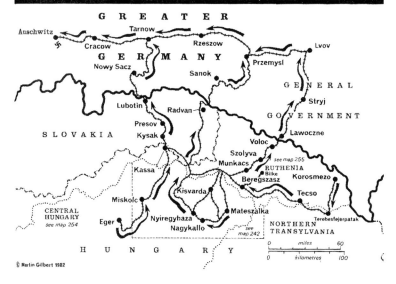

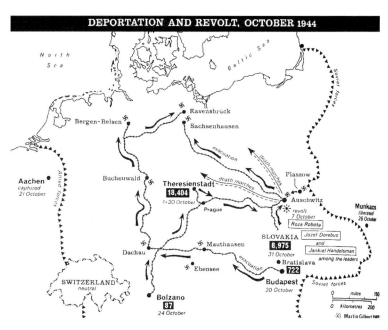

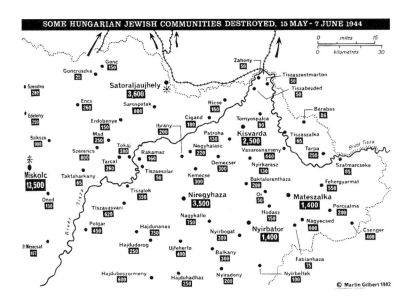

SOME HUNGARIAN JEWISH COMMUNITIES DESTROYED, 15 MAY - 7 JUNE 1944

© Martin Gilbert 1982

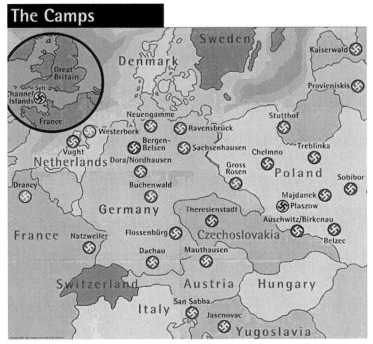

The Camps

After staying in the ghetto in Mátészalka, my grandmother, her family, and many other Hungarian Jews were deported, mostly to Auschwitz, on these packed cattle cars.

View of the entrance to the main camp of Auschwitz. These are the gates of the concentration camp Auschwitz. Auschwitz was responsible for the death of many Jewish people and other innocent victims during the Holocaust. The gate reads *Arbeit Macht Frei,* which means "Work Makes One Free." The Nazis wanted to fool the prisoners into believing that if they worked hard and did what they were told, they would be set free. In actuality, this sign meant nothing. The ultimate goal of the camp was to murder all Jews entirely.

Bergen-Belsen, a concentration camp in Germany, was the final camp that my grandmother was taken to during the Holocaust. The giant pile in the background is a heap of dead bodies, stacked so high that the dead greatly outnumbered the living. At Bergen-Belsen my grandmother watched her cousin and sister die and then be thrown onto the pile.

These are the barracks at Bergen-Belsen, seen shortly after liberation. Here prisoners walked around aimlessly, fighting to survive with the last bit of hope that they could hold onto.

6,000 naked prisoners are assembled in the courtyard of the Mauthausen concentration camp where they await disinfection.

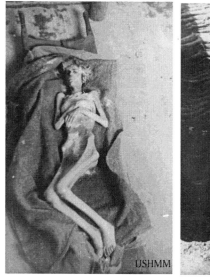

(l) An emaciated female survivor who has just been disinfected lies on a stretcher in Bergen-Belsen. (r) Corpses in a mass grave at Mauthausen.

View of a barracks at the Plaszow concentration camp. Prisoners at Plaszow concentration camp in Krakow, Poland, were forced to do strenuous labor in the excruciatingly hot summer months. Here, my grandmother and the other prisoners were ordered to build a swimming pool for the officers. They carried massive rocks up a hill and were often beaten or whipped. These beatings happened on a daily basis if the officers felt the prisoners were not working fast enough, or more often than not, for no reason at all.

 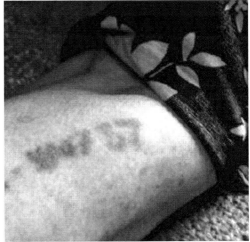

(l) Elizabeth Goldstein showing the tattoo from Auschwitz.
(r) Close up of the tattoo—A-20737.

(l) Replica of the metal comb, similar to the comb Elizabeth found while walking to the munitions factory. She used the comb to style the girls' hair that was beginning to grow back. (r) Open Hebrew Prayer book—read from back to front.

(l) Notations of parents' and siblings' birthdays. Elizabeth wrote them in while she was in hospital in Sweden, so she would not forget. (r) Hebrew Prayer book, given to Elizabeth in Sweden by the Hebrew Immigrant Aid Society (HIAS).

Elizabeth Goldstein, honored in May 2005, at the Camden Waterfront at a candlelighting ceremony on the Battleship New Jersey (formerly USS New Jersey—most decorated battleship in World War II; now a museum).

Caption: l to r—Fogarty family: Shana, Bryana (sister), Adam (brother), Elizabeth Goldstein, Joseph (father), and Susan (mother) in May 2005.

Three generations; l to r—Elizabeth, Shana, and Susan (mother).

Endnotes

1 **Plaszow** At first, Plaszow was a labor camp policed by Ukrainian guards. By 1944 it had become a concentration camp controlled by the SS (Harran 23).

2 **Hundsfeld** (means "dog's field") was a forced labor camp near Breslau, at the time, part of Germany. Today this city is part of Poland.

3 **Gross-Rosen** Formerly a satellite camp of Sachsenhausen, Gross-Rosen, Germany, became an independent camp on May 1, 1941 (Harran 229). The camp was known for its huge stone quarry.

4 **Mauthausen** "A few weeks after the occupation of Austria by German troops, high-ranking German SS and police officers visited the Mauthausen quarries and found them to be a suitable location for a concentration camp. On August 8, 1938, prisoners from the Dachau concentration camp were transferred to the "Wiener Graben" quarry and construction of the Mauthausen concentration camp was begun. The Mauthausen camp was the central camp (referred to as the "mother camp" by the SS guards) for all of Austria. Forty-nine permanent subcamps, as well as some temporary ones that existed only for a few weeks, were administered from the Mauthausen camp. Between August 8, 1938, and liberation on May 5, 1945, some 195,000 persons of both sexes were imprisoned in these camps." –www.jewishvirtuallibrary.org

5 **Muselman** "German term meaning 'Muslim,' widely used by concentration camp prisoners to refer to inmates who were on

the verge of death from starvation, exhaustion, and despair. A person who had reached the Muselman stage had little, if any, chance for survival and usually died within weeks. The origin of the term is unclear."
www. History.ucsb.edu/projects/Holocaust

[6]**Bergen-Belsen** "Bergen-Belsen was a concentration camp near Hanover in northwest Germany, located between the villages of Bergen and Belsen. Built in 1940, it was a prisoner-of-war camp for French and Belgium prisoners. In 1941, it was renamed Stalag 311 and housed about 20,000 Russian prisoners. The camp changed its name to Bergen-Belsen and was converted into a concentration camp in 1943. Jews with foreign passports were kept there to be exchanged for German nationals imprisoned abroad, although very few exchanges were made. About 200 Jews were allowed to immigrate to Palestine and about 1,500 Hungarian Jews were allowed to immigrate to Switzerland, both took place under the rubric of exchanges for German nationals.

Bergen-Belsen mainly served as a holding camp for the Jewish prisoners. The camp was divided into eight sections, a detention camp, two women's camps, a special camp, neutrals camps, "star" camp (mainly Dutch prisoners who wore a Star of David on their clothing instead of the camp uniform), Hungarian camp and a tent camp. It was designed to hold 10,000 prisoners, however, by the war's end more than 60,000 prisoners were detained there, due to the large numbers of those evacuated from Auschwitz and other camps from the East. Tens of thousands of prisoners from other camps came to Bergen-Belsen after agonizing death marches." –www.jewishvirtuallibrary.org

[7] **Marie Magdalene "Marlene" Dietrich** (December 27, 1901-May 6, 1992), also known as **Maria Magdalena Dietrich,** was a German actress, entertainer, and singer. "Dietrich became an American citizen in 1937, raised a record number of war bonds and entertained American troops during the Second World War. Dietrich was a staunch anti-Nazi who despised Germany's anti-

Semitic policies of the time. Her singing helped on the homefront of the U.S.A too, as she recorded a number of anti-Nazi records in German for the OSS. Including recording *Lili Marleen*, a curious example of a song transcending the hatreds of war." www.wikipedia.org

[8]**Pastor Martin Niemoeller** Pastor Niemoeller was the leader of the anti-Nazi Confessing Church in Germany. Because of his arrest for "attacking the state," he was sent to a concentration camp as a "personal prisoner." According to his widow, Sibil Niemoeller, the quoted poem are his exact words.—from "What did Pastor Martin Niemoeller Really Say"

Works Cited

Bachrach, Susan. *Tell Them We Remember*. Boston: Little Brown, 1994.

Bulow, Louis. "Swedish Portraits." *Man of Courage*. 1986. 4 Aug. 2004 <http://www.auschwitz.dk/Wallenberg.htm>.

Gilbert, Martin. *Atlas of the Holocaust*. New York: Morrow, 1993.

Goldstein, Elizabeth Blum. Personal interview. 20 June 2004 to 19 Mar. 2005.

Harran, Marilyn, et al. *The Holocaust Chronicle*. Chicago: International Publications, 2002.

"History of Hungary." World History at KMLA. *Return to Stability under the Horthy Regime, 1921-1939*. 2000. 20 Mar. 2005 <http://www.zum.de/whkmla/region/eceurope/hungary192139.html>

"Hungary." *Encyclopedia of the Holocaust*. 1990.

"Hungary: General Survey." *Encyclopedia of the Holocaust*. 1990.

"Hungary: Jews During the Holocaust." *Macmillan Encyclopedia of the Holocaust*. 1990.

"Maps and Photos." United States Holocaust Memorial Museum. 20 Mar. 2005 <http://www.ushmm.org>.